Curing Leadership Insomnia

Curing Leadership Insomnia

How to Use the *Truby Management System* To Fix What Keeps You Up at Night

By Bill & Joann Truby

Spoiler Alert: The ultimate sleep-stealer for insomniac leaders? **People problems.** This book gives you the blueprint to not only fix your team but also untangle every process issue dragging down their performance.

Curing Leadership Insomnia

Bill & Joann Truby

Published by Angel's Dream Publishing Company
P.O. Box 1440
Mt. Shasta, California 96067

Find us on the World Wide Web at https://trubyachievements.com

Copyright: © 2024 by Bill & Joann Truby and Truby Achievements, Inc.
Cover design: Elizabeth Diane, Lucid 9 Design

Colophon
This book was created with Adobe InDesign 2025. The fonts used are Lato and Myriad Pro.

Notice of Rights
All rights reserved. No part of this book may be reproduced or transmitted in any form or by any means, electronic, mechanical, photocopying, recording, or otherwise, without the prior written permission of the publisher. For information on getting permission for reprints and excerpts, contact Bill Truby at Truby Achievements, Inc.

Notice of Liability
The information in this book is published on an "as is" basis without warranty. While every precaution has been taken in the preparation of this book, neither the author, the editor, or Truby Achievements, Inc. shall have any liability to any person or entity with respect to any loss or damage caused or alleged to be caused directly or indirectly by any information in this book.

ISBN 979-8-218-53905-4
Printed and bound in the United States.

Dedication

Thanks... Tanya Bumstead Quinn

This book, plus every operational detail of our business could not exist were it not for our friend and COO, Tanya. She works tirelessly, cares completely, and believes intensely in the mission of our company.

Thank you, Tanya. Without you, we would still be in the dark ages of business operations – using dial-up internet and sending flyers through the mail. You are the partner that makes our business fly!

Warmly,

Bill & Joann Truby

Table of Contents

Prologue: A Primer on the *Truby Managements System (TMS)* Management System...1

Section 1. What You Need to Know First

Chapter 1. Introduction 5
Chapter 2. Why Fixing Your Team is So Important......................11
Chapter 3. Why Bill Truby Has What It Takes to Help YOU.........19
Chapter 4. Joann Truby - the Soul of the Company and an Astounding Coach 23

Section 2. TMS Phase One: Transform (Laying the Foundation for Success)

Chapter 5. Phase One Introduction 29
Chapter 6. Step One: Building a Foundation Through Team Bonding..31
Chapter 7. Step Two: The Power of Agreements in Team Dynamics..41

Section 3. TMS Phase Two: Organize (Creating Clarity and Accountability)

Chapter 8. Phase Two Introduction......................................51
Chapter 9. Step Three: Establishing Structure for a High-Performing Team...53
Chapter 10. Step Four: Clarifying Expectations with Role/Responsibility Sheets 63

Section 4. TMS Phase Three: Mobilize (Turning Strategy into Action)

Chapter 11. Phase Three Introduction 73
Chapter 12. Step Five: Understanding and Delivering the Value 75
Chapter 13. Step Six: The Power of Goals in Achieving Team Success...83

Section 5. TMS Phase Four: Optimize (Laying the Foundation for Success)
    Chapter 14. Phase Four Introduction 93
    Chapter 15. Step Seven: The Power of Efficiency Systems 95
    Chapter 16. Step Eight: The Mindset and Practice of Continuous Improvement 103

Section 6. Conclusion
    Chapter 17. Putting It All Together 113
    Chapter 18. What's Next? How the TMS Can Help YOU 117

Section 7. Appendices
    Appendix A. Types of Team Problems *Truby Management System* Can Solve 125
    Appendix B. Rationale for Using the *Truby Management System* 131

Prologue:
A Primer on the *Truby Management System (TMS)*

Welcome to **Curing Leadership Insomnia**, where you'll discover how the *Truby Management System (TMS)* can fix what keeps you up at night.

If you're a leader who spends sleepless nights worrying about your team's performance, unresolved conflict, or never-ending people problems, this book is for you. It's designed to give you a clear understanding of the *Truby Management System* and how it can provide practical, real-world solutions to the leadership challenges that keep you awake.

Before you dive in, it's important to understand that this book is a primer—a foundational teaching and treatment for each of the eight steps of the *Truby Management System*.

Each chapter will give you an overview of one of the steps in the *Truby Management System*, showing you how to implement basic elements of the system and offering actionable strategies for each step that you can apply immediately. The goal is to give you a taste of the power of the *Truby Management System*—how it can help fix the people problems that sap your energy, and how it can transform your leadership approach from reactive to proactive.

Why This Book Is Just the Beginning

This book is your entry point into a system that has helped leaders worldwide. By reading this book, you'll gain valuable insights and start fixing some of the most common problems leaders face.

But if you want to truly cure your leadership insomnia—if you want to master the art of leading a high-performing team with confidence and clarity, knowing how to confidently handle ANY issue that can come up while building your team and maintaining their performance—then the full *Truby Management System* training is the key to your success.

While this book provides a solid introduction to the *Truby Management System*, it's only the starting point. The real transformational experience comes with the full training. Each step of the system is more complex than it might seem on the surface, and fully mastering these concepts requires deeper training and practice.

The *Truby Management System* is practical, proven, and designed to address the real-world issues that leaders face every day. So, read this book, apply what you learn, and then, when you're ready for the full transformation, take the next step by accessing our complete training curriculum. Let us help you sleep soundly, knowing your team is performing at its best.

Access the full training curriculum at
https://TrubyAchievements.com.

SECTION 1

WHAT YOU NEED TO KNOW FIRST

Chapter 1.
Introduction

Leadership isn't for the faint of heart. As a leader, you've likely experienced the exhilaration of building something great—a business, a team, a product, or a vision. But alongside that excitement comes a quiet, persistent pressure. You know the feeling: the meetings that spiral into conflict, the passive-aggressive behavior that poisons collaboration, the frustration of repeating the same instructions over and over without seeing results.

Then, there are those nights. The ones where sleep escapes you. You lie awake, staring at the ceiling, replaying the conversations, conflicts, and unproductive meetings in your head, wondering how to finally get your team to work well together. It's not uncommon. **You're not alone.**

The **number one reason leaders lose sleep isn't strategy, budgets, or market challenges—it is people problems**. Whether it's clashing personalities, poor communication, low morale, missed goals, or lack of accountability, dysfunctional teams are the thorn in the side of even the best leaders. **And this is the very problem that this book, using the proven** *Truby Management System***, will help you fix.**

The Testimonial That Inspired This Book

Let me share the story of Greg, one of our clients who epitomizes the type of leadership insomnia we aim to cure. Greg managed a successful mid-sized company. On the surface, everything looked fine—the business was profitable, they had experienced steady growth, and his team was filled with talented people. Yet Greg was exhausted and frustrated beyond belief. His problem? **The team wasn't working together.**

Despite their individual skills, they weren't aligned. Miscommunication was rampant, projects got delayed, and conflict simmered just beneath the surface. As Greg put it, "It felt like I was playing whack-a-mole with problems every day. For every issue I fixed, two more would pop up. I'd lie awake at night thinking about everything that could go wrong the next day—and most of it came back to my people." He tried every leadership tip and management fad he could find, but nothing seemed to stick.

Then Greg discovered the *Truby Management System*. By following the step-by-step process—starting with bonding his team, creating clear agreements, and defining roles—Greg saw an immediate shift. His people began working together more smoothly. Accountability improved, meetings became more productive, and conflict was resolved constructively. Within months, Greg's team had transformed from a group of individuals into a cohesive, high-performing unit.

"I never thought it could feel this good to lead," Greg said. "I used to wake up in the middle of the night dreading the next day. Now I sleep soundly because I know my team can handle whatever comes our way. They've got each other's backs—and they've got mine too."

This is the transformation we want to bring to **your leadership and your team** through this book.

Why People Problems Are the Real Problem

Greg's story is not unique. Whether you lead a small business, a corporate team, or a nonprofit organization, the chances are high that **people problems are the most significant source of your frustration.** Research shows that **leaders spend up to 70% of their time dealing with people issues**—whether it's conflict resolution, managing poor performance, or trying to motivate disengaged employees. That's time you could be spending on strategic initiatives, growing your business, or, frankly, just enjoying life.

The truth is, **most people problems don't fix themselves.** Hoping that the team will magically improve over time is a recipe for endless frustration. Dysfunctional teams remain dysfunctional unless the leader steps in to actively address the core issues. But here's the good news: **you can fix these problems**—and you don't have to do it alone.

The *Truby Management System* offers a **proven pathway to turn struggling teams into high-performing, well-oiled machines.** Whether your team is drowning in conflict or just needs fine-tuning, this system will give you the tools to **eliminate dysfunction, create alignment, and build accountability.**

This book will walk you through the **four phases of transformation—Transform, Organize, Mobilize, and Optimize—** and give you an inside look at the **eight essential steps** that will fix your team from the ground up.

What You Can Expect from This Book

We understand that you're busy. Your days are packed with meetings, deadlines, and decisions. You don't have time for complex theories or vague management advice. That's why **this book is designed to be practical and actionable.** You'll walk away with **specific tools and strategies** you can implement right away to start seeing results.

Here's a quick overview of what we'll cover:

- **Phase 1: Transform** – You'll learn how to build trust and strong relationships within your team. We'll explore the power of bonding and mutual agreements as the foundation of teamwork.

- **Phase 2: Organize** – We'll help you bring clarity and structure to your team by defining roles, responsibilities, and expectations. Everyone will know what they're accountable for—and to whom.

- **Phase 3: Mobilize** – We'll show you how to align your team's efforts around your company's core value and set meaningful goals. Your team will move forward with purpose and focus.

- **Phase 4: Optimize** – You'll discover how to implement efficiency systems that streamline your workflows, boost productivity, and create a culture of continuous improvement.

Along the way, you'll learn **how to manage conflict constructively, communicate clearly, and create systems that make your work easier**. Most importantly, you'll discover how to **lead with confidence**—knowing you have the tools to handle any challenge your team throws your way.

The Results You Can Expect

What will your life look like after implementing the *Truby Management System*? Here's what leaders who've gone through the program have experienced:

- **Reduced stress and more restful nights** – No more waking up at 3 a.m. wondering how to handle the latest conflict or missed deadline.

- **A stronger, more cohesive team** – Your people will work together seamlessly, trust each other, and take ownership of their work.

- **More time to focus on what matters** – You'll spend less time managing people problems and more time driving strategic initiatives.

- **Increased productivity and profitability** – When your team functions smoothly, output increases and the bottom line improves.

- **A renewed passion for leadership** – Leading a high-performing team isn't just easier—it's more enjoyable. You'll rediscover the joy of leadership and the satisfaction of making a meaningful impact.

Section 1. What You Need to Know First

Why This Book Matters Now

In today's fast-paced business environment, **effective leadership is more important than ever**. Whether you're facing rapid growth, unexpected challenges, or a shifting market, the success of your organization depends on your ability to **lead a high-performing team**.

The good news is **you don't have to figure it all out on your own**. This book, built on the proven principles of the *Truby Management System*, will give you the roadmap you need to fix your team, eliminate people problems, and become the leader your organization deserves.

So, if you're ready to **cure your leadership insomnia**, transform your team, and lead with confidence—let's get started. Your **journey to stress-free leadership and a high-performing team** begins here.

Chapter 2.
Why Fixing Your Team is So Important

As a leader, you've probably heard the phrase "people problems" more times than you care to count. Whether it's interpersonal conflict, low morale, lack of accountability, or general underperformance, people issues seem to be the thorn in every leader's side. In fact, you might feel like managing these issues takes up more time than the actual work your team is meant to do.

Bob was struggling with his print shop. He maintained a good reputation with the people of the community because he constantly participated in community events. People knew Bob. People wanted to give Bob their business. And they did. He received an abundance of orders.

But when it came to delivering the variety of print services he offered, he was wearily not successful. His ten employees were always late. They bickered amongst each other. They were not performing to their capacity, and certainly not doing the kind of quality job Bob promised to his customers. In short, Bob felt like he was pushing a string uphill when trying to get the work done. He was stressed to the max, not making much money, and his business processes were suffering. He had a team that needed to be fixed. But he didn't know what to do. Yet, ironically, that's what he spent most of his time on – people problems.

Here's the hard truth: **teams don't fix themselves—leaders do**. And that's where the *Truby Management System (TMS)* comes in. This book is your gateway to understanding how you, as a leader, can eliminate people problems and transform your team into a high-performing unit. The solutions don't come from waiting for the team to magically improve. They come from proactive leadership equipped with the right tools, strategies, and systems.

People Problems: Why They Persist

It's common for leaders to feel overwhelmed by the constant "people issues" on their teams. From low accountability to recurring mistakes, negative behaviors crop up time and time again. Many try to fix these problems by addressing them individually—like playing a game of "whack-a-mole." You might put out one fire only for another to flare up in its place.

The reality is, these symptoms all stem from a deeper root cause: a lack of true teamwork. When a team is fragmented, the natural result is dysfunction in its many forms. That's where most leaders get stuck, dealing with the surface-level symptoms rather than addressing the core issue of **team dynamics**.

The Truby Management System: A Proven Fix

The *Truby Management System (TMS)* is a game-changer. Over 40 years of implementation in businesses of all sizes has proven that this system can dramatically reduce—and often eliminate—people problems. From Fortune 500 companies to small businesses, the TMS has consistently transformed teams by focusing on eight simple, yet profound steps.

This system works because it's not a complex, time-consuming program that you must pause your work to implement. Instead, it's a **mind shift** in how you think and lead. You learn how to do what you're already doing—just differently and more effectively. It's based on ancient principles of success, yet designed for modern leadership, enabling you to see rapid, lasting improvements.

A Leadership Mindset: The Foundation of a High-Performing Team

Here's another critical insight: **success starts with the mindset of the leader.** The *Truby Management System* teaches you to adopt a **leadership mindset**—one that focuses not just on task management, but on leading accountable people through clear agreements and valued deliverables. With this mindset in place, the rest of the system provides the infrastructure to ensure your team operates smoothly.

Leadership is more than solving problems; it's about setting a direction and ensuring your team follows. With the TMS, you'll learn to create effective interactions, clear **structures**, foster accountability, and establish effective communication patterns that help prevent people problems from surfacing in the first place.

The Eight Steps of the Truby Management System

In this book, we'll walk you through the eight critical steps of the *Truby Management System*:

1. **Team Bonding**: Building strong connections among team members is foundational to success.
2. **Agreements**: Establishing clear agreements on how the team functions prevents misunderstandings and aligns energy and effort.

3. **Structure**: Defining roles and responsibilities creates clarity and avoids overlap.
4. **Responsibilities**: Ensuring everyone knows what they're accountable for helps avoid missteps, redundancy, turf battles, and improves team efficiency
5. **Value Alignment**: Aligning your team with the value your organization delivers to customers, clients, or patients is essential to conduct cohesive operations.
6. **Goals**: Setting clear goals ensures everyone is working toward a common purpose.
7. **Systems**: Creating efficient systems streamlines operations, minimizes wasted time and effort, and improves productivity and profitability .
8. **Continuous Improvement**: Building a culture of improvement keeps your team competitive while evolving and performing at its peak.

The eight steps of the *Truby Management System* are implemented sequentially in four phases: Transform, Organize, Mobilize, and Optimize.

> **Transform:** If a team doesn't transform into something different, it will remain the same – with the same dynamics, behaviors, and problems. Transforming a group of individuals into a high-performing team it the necessary first phase of team and organizational development. Remember, people drive process.
>
> **Organize:** A transformed group of team members needs to be organized. Even a group of volunteers must sort out who is responsible for what. An organized team has clarity of roles and responsibilities. Boundaries are clear, and every aspect of what the team is to achieve is

"owned" by a given role. Organization provides structure upon which operational success can be built.

Mobilize: After people are transformed into a team and organized into a clear structure with clarity of responsibility and outcomes, there needs to be movement towards achievement. In this phase, the team focuses on and aligns with the value underpinning the product or service the team delivers. There is also a clarity of direction and goals. The team has movement that is defined and aligned.

Optimize: High-performing teams aren't satisfied with achieving. They want to do so smoothly, without wasted effort, time, or resources. In this phase, the team ensures they are doing all they can in the best way they can. They align around efficiency systems and seek continuous improvement.

This is the essence of the *Truby Management System* – four phases, two steps in each phase.

Here is how the roadmap looks:

Transform:

- **Team Bonding**
- **Agreements**

Organize:

- **Structure**
- **Responsibilities**

Mobilize

- Value Alignment
- Goals

Optimize:

- Systems
- Continuous Improvement

Why Teams Don't Fix Themselves

The truth is, **people issues will continue to surface until you, as a leader, intervene with the right mindset and tools.** The *Truby Management System* offers you those tools. It's not just another management philosophy or a one-size-fits-all program. It's a **system** designed to fit into your daily leadership practices, providing immediate, tangible results.

As you read this book, you'll begin to see how each step contributes to solving people problems, boosting morale, and driving your team to higher performance levels. And the best part? These changes don't require massive overhauls. With the TMS, you'll learn how to make small, strategic adjustments that create powerful results.

You'll also get a glimpse into how this practical and commonsense system increases morale, retention, company growth, and team performance – while decreasing turnover, time-consuming interpersonal issues, and cumbersome operational practices.

As you learn more about the *Truby Management System*, you will notice that it all starts with fixing, building, or enhancing your team. The TMS is a "people first" approach to success. Why is this? Because the goal of any organization is for people to use processes to deliver a product or service to clients or customers for mutual reward.

> **Organizations consist of people using process to deliver a product or serve to statisfied clients or customers for mutual reward.**

If a leader or manager tries to fix the processes or business practices within an organization without addressing the people component, it's like increasing the horsepower of a car with flat tires. It's still not going to run well. Truby's commonsense approach believes people drive process. If you fix the people, the processes almost automatically fix themselves.

Remember print shop Bob? He put the TMS into place, focusing on fixing the people first, and within 3 months, his team began functioning effectively. Workflow was smooth. People problems were essentially nonexistent. Moreover, those same 10 people were yielding 160% of the work they produced just a few months before. Their morale was high, and they came to work on time! Bob was less stressed, less weary, and was excited to come to work. Now, it was fun!

What do I do after I read this book?

This book is just the beginning. Once you experience the transformation the *Truby Management System* brings to your leadership and your team, you'll understand why leaders worldwide have embraced it. If you're serious about fixing your team for good and eliminating the frustration of constant people problems, then the full **Truby Management System training** is your next logical step.

By the end of this book, you'll have a foundational understanding of the system and its benefits. But to truly unlock the full potential of your leadership and team, consider diving deeper with our comprehensive training programs. You'll gain access to detailed tutorials, assessments, and additional tools to fully implement the system and lead your team to lasting success. You'll also be equipped with the knowledge and power to slay any issue that comes up, threatening to sidetrack you.

Sound good? Just remember this – Teams don't fix themselves; leaders do. So it all starts with you. It starts with leadership. Decide to make a difference, and you can. We'll take the journey together.

But first, let's look at the authors of this popular and successful system, Bill & Joann Truby. You should get to know who you are learning from. They are the co-founders of Truby Achievements, Inc. They both bring brilliant and valuable content to the table. The following chapters provide a little bit about your guides.

Chapter 3.
Why Bill Truby Has What It Takes to Help YOU

Bottom line? Bill fixes teams – quickly, with sustainable results. He can give YOU the "Leadership Expertise to Transform Teams."

But how does he do it?

Bill's extensive experience in counseling, team management, and leadership training has shaped the *Truby Management System* (TMS), a proven framework that takes leaders step by step through processes that not only fix broken teams but also enhance successful ones. The TMS has been successfully applied across various industries, including healthcare, hospitality, manufacturing, and professional services firms to name a few.

With over 40 years of experience, Bill Truby has become a leading expert in team dynamics, leadership development, and business process performance. Armed with a BA in Theology and an MA in Psychology, Bill combines deep insights into human behavior with a practical, no-nonsense approach to leadership. His career spans decades of helping businesses—ranging from small startups to Fortune 500 companies—build high-performing teams, resolve conflict, and achieve outstanding results.

Why Bill Truby's Approach Works

What sets Bill apart is his ability to create commonsense tools that are easy to implement but highly effective. The *Truby Management System* (TMS) doesn't require leaders to overhaul their entire operations. Instead, it encourages leaders to work smarter by doing things they are already doing differently, using strategies that fit seamlessly into their existing workflows while driving remarkable improvements. Leaders and teams alike are often surprised by how quickly they see results once they implement the TMS.

Bill's approach is rooted in ancient wisdom about human behavior and team dynamics, but his training is anything but outdated. It's practical, realistic, and proven to work in the modern business landscape. Whether you're facing issues like lack of accountability, low morale, poor communication, passive-aggressive behavior, or inefficient meetings, Bill Truby's system provides the tools to fix these problems effectively.

The Real-World Impact of Bill Truby's Work

Throughout his career, Bill has consistently transformed struggling teams into cohesive, high-performing units. One notable success involved a large hotel and casino in Reno, Nevada, where implementing the TMS led to a 30% increase in net profit within one year without the need for major capital investments. Similarly, his work with a marine construction company helped them identify the true value they were delivering to clients—risk management, not just lowest-bid construction services—leading to a significant increase in profitability as the company realigned its focus.

Bill's clients often say his training is more practical than an MBA, addressing the real-life challenges leaders face on a day-to-day basis. This is because his methods focus on resolving issues that directly affect team dynamics, productivity, and business profitability.

Personal Growth for Leaders

Bill often says, "Teams don't fix themselves – leaders do!" But, he says, "Most leaders live with a secret – they don't know how to lead." He explains how most leaders have been promoted because of great work ethics, an engaging personality, or great performance as a line worker but have never been trained in leadership and management. He points out that leadership demands a whole new set of skills than the newly promoted person has. A great architect designer doesn't automatically have the skills to conduct good project management.

It's a commonsense notion that Bill Truby illuminates when he explains how a leader, who wants to fix a troubled team or develop an existing team, needs three categories of training – 1) A catalogue of topics, systems, and processes that are critical to building a high-performing team, 2) The skills needed to assess a team, train a team, and a toolkit to handle any of the obstacles and speed bumps that inevitably sneak into the leader and team's work day, and 3) Personal mastery, confidence, and a healthy wellbeing.

A leader does not leave himself or herself at home. Yet, when that leader arrives to begin interacting with the team, the level of function (or dysfunction) will be directly overlaid onto every interaction, communication, and behavior that the leader performs.

So, beyond improving team performance, Bill's training also emphasizes personal leadership growth. Leaders who go through the full TMS training often report not just professional success, but also increased personal fulfillment. They gain confidence in their leadership abilities, experience less stress, and enjoy the process of leading more. This personal transformation is a core part of Bill's mission: to create confident, capable leaders who can run their teams effectively, solve problems before they escalate, and achieve lasting success.

In short, Bill Truby's experience, wisdom, and practical approach provide leaders with everything they need to transform their teams, enhance business performance, and achieve both personal and professional success.

That's why Bill Truby has what it takes to help YOU!

What about Joann Truby? What does she bring to the table?

Chapter 4.
Joann Truby – the Soul of the Company and an Astounding Coach

Joann and Bill began working together in 1997. Though Bill is brilliant at creating and presenting the content in a practical, commonsense, and easy-to-learn manner, Joann's influence runs deeper. She brings to the success of Truby Achievements her amazing ability to coach to success, using her wisdom and skills for the company as well as those receiving training from Truby Achievements.

Joann Truby's journey into the world of coaching is more than just a career; it is a narrative woven with passion, precision, and an innate ability to bring out the best in people. Even before age 30, Joann had already built a distinguished reputation as an athlete and world-class coach, shaping champions with the same techniques she would later apply in the professional realm. As a national roller-skating champion, her early life was immersed in the principles of dedication, discipline, and resilience—qualities that would become cornerstones of her coaching philosophy.

Joann's life took a new trajectory when she co-founded **Truby Achievements, Inc.**, alongside her husband, Bill Truby. Their shared vision was simple yet profound: help people become confident, successful leaders through actionable tools grounded in common sense and timeless truths. Central to their approach is the *Truby Management System (TMS)*, which emphasizes shifting mindsets to unlock sustainable personal and team growth. Joann's role in this venture goes beyond delivering knowledge—her magic lies in creating a transformation that feels both natural and deeply personal.

Section 1. What You Need to Know First

What makes Joann a remarkable coach is her mastery of intuition. Described as having a "process-driven, intuitive wisdom," Joann knows exactly what to say and—more importantly—when to say nothing at all. This ability to adapt her approach in the moment sets her apart from the typical coach. She applies a blend of structured feedback and spontaneous insight, allowing each interaction to be not just effective but also meaningful. Her clients, regardless of position or stress levels, rarely cancel their sessions, demonstrating the trust and anticipation her presence fosters.

Joann believes that **coaching is not about telling people what to do, but about helping them discover their own best solutions**. One of the core elements of her method involves acting as a mirror, reflecting the truth without judgment or bias. This approach enables clients to see their blind spots clearly and address the underlying behaviors that may hinder their growth. Her coaching is a journey of self-awareness, where clients learn to own their choices and behaviors, a principle Joann has honed through her life experiences.

For Joann, **every coaching relationship is a partnership**, a process of co-creation where she crafts personalized programs tailored to meet individual needs. Whether a leader seeks to become a better communicator, a team member wants to navigate conflicts, or an executive aspires to manage stress effectively, Joann's strategies are always practical and actionable. The Truby Achievements philosophy stresses not doing "different things" but "doing things differently," aligning effort with natural laws to achieve sustainable outcomes.

Her commitment to coaching goes beyond formal sessions. Joann lives by the philosophy of lifelong learning and sharing wisdom. This ethos is embedded in the community she has built through Truby Achievements, where members continually pass on what they've learned, fostering an ecosystem of growth and mutual support.

Through Joann's guidance, leaders are not just trained but transformed. She equips them with the tools to become mentors themselves, empowering them to inspire those around them. This ripple effect is at the heart of her legacy: **helping individuals not only become their best but also enabling them to help others do the same**. Her work is a testament to the belief that great coaching doesn't just improve performance—it elevates the whole person, nurturing confidence, clarity, and connection.

Joann Truby's coaching journey is a dynamic narrative that showcases the art of unlocking human potential. Her clients walk away not just with solutions, but with a sense of ownership over their paths forward. And in the process, Joann continues to demonstrate that coaching, when done well, is both a science and an art—a delicate dance between knowledge, insight, and heart.

SECTION 2

TMS PHASE ONE: TRANSFORM

Laying the Foundation for Success

Chapter 5.
Phase One Introduction: *Transform - Laying the Foundation for Success*

Every journey begins with a first step. When building a high-performing team, that first step is transformation. In the *Truby Management System*, the **Transform** phase focuses on laying the foundational elements that will empower your team to work together cohesively, build trust, and develop a sense of shared purpose. Without this foundation, no amount of strategy, goals, or systems will create the results you're after.

But what does transformation really mean in a team context? It's about taking individual contributors and turning them into a high-performing, united team. This transformation begins with the essential human connection—bonding. When your team members bond, they understand each other's strengths and weaknesses. They develop trust, which eliminates the common barriers like gossip, miscommunication, or competition. This bond becomes the glue that holds your team together, allowing them to tackle any challenge collaboratively.

The *Truby Management System* starts here because without trust and bonding, nothing else works. Leaders often think their team just needs better systems or clearer goals, but in reality the lack of interpersonal connection is usually at the heart of dysfunction. By focusing on transformation, you're not just changing the way your team works—you're changing the way they relate to one another. You're creating a space where collaboration flourishes and where people genuinely care about the team's success.

The Transform phase also incorporates agreements—the rules by which your team will operate. These aren't top-down mandates. Instead, these are mutual agreements that the team collectively creates, ensuring everyone knows how to communicate, handle conflict, and support one another. These agreements lay the groundwork for everything that comes next, enabling the team to operate in alignment rather than chaos.

Transformation is about creating a shift—not just in how your team works, but in how they think and feel. Once this foundation is in place, your team will be ready to take on the challenges ahead with confidence and unity.

Truby Management System Steps for Phase One: Transform

- Bonding
- Agreements

Chapter 6.
Step One: Building a Foundation Through Team Bonding

To build a high-performing team, the first and most essential step is **bonding**. Whether in personal relationships or professional environments, trust and rapport are the foundation for success. Without a solid bond, communication falters, collaboration weakens, and people start to work in silos instead of as a unified team. Bonding is the key that unlocks the potential for a team to not only function but to thrive.

In leadership, this truth is amplified. When a team is not bonded, it becomes difficult—if not impossible—to fix the deeper issues plaguing performance. That's why, in the *Truby Management System (TMS)*, bonding is the very first step. It is the first building block on the road to fixing a troubled team and setting them on the path to success. Sometimes, taking a team through the bonding process automatically fixes a host of other problems.

Yvonne, a nurse and clinic manager, struggled for three years after she got promoted to this leadership role. When she conducted the "Team Profile Bonding" exercise detailed in the full TMS online training, she was awe-struck by how powerful the process was for her team. She could see a difference the very next morning. Her team members commented on how they could feel the difference. Within days, various employees expressed, "Now it's fun to come to work!"

Why Bonding Matters in Teams

A sense of belonging and connection is not just nice to have—it's critical for teamwork. People are social creatures by nature, and this desire to connect and belong exists in every environment. When team members feel a connection to one another, they are more willing to collaborate, communicate openly, and work towards common goals.

Research has shown that teams with strong bonds:

- **Perform better:** There is greater alignment, increased morale, and fewer mistakes.

- **Experience higher retention rates**: Bonded teams have more stability because people want to stay where they feel valued and connected.

- **Exhibit fewer interpersonal issues**: Trust and understanding between team members prevent miscommunications and conflicts from spiraling into bigger problems.

- **Achieve measurable improvements in complaints, sick days, and negative talk**: When people are bonded, they are also emotionally invested in the team's performance and environment.

A team that isn't bonded will struggle with internal divisions and lack a cohesive vision, leading to poor collaboration and frequent misunderstandings.

What Causes a Lack of Bonding?

Teams often fail to bond due to a variety of factors, including:

1. **Lack of Trust:** If team members don't trust each other, they'll keep interactions minimal, focusing only on the task at hand without the willingness to engage more deeply.

2. **Poor Communication:** When communication is inconsistent or unclear, it creates confusion and misalignment, driving wedges between team members.

3. **Undefined Roles and Responsibilities:** Without clarity on who is responsible for what, team members are prone to stepping on each other's toes or leaving gaps in the work. This breeds frustration and erodes trust.

4. **Competing Priorities:** If individual team members are focused more on their own goals rather than the team's shared objectives, this division can lead to resentment and disengagement.

5. **Leadership Gaps:** When leaders don't actively cultivate a sense of bonding among their team, members are left to figure out how to work together on their own. Often, this leads to cliques, exclusion, and lack of cohesion.

The Consequences of a Non-Bonded Team

The effects of poor bonding are profound. Here are the key consequences:

- **Low Morale:** Team members feel isolated and disconnected, which leads to dissatisfaction at work. Low morale can spread quickly and bring down overall productivity.

- **Increased Conflict:** Without strong relationships in place, minor disagreements can quickly escalate into major conflicts. A lack of understanding and empathy can cause frustration to fester.

- **Higher Turnover:** Employees who don't feel connected to their team are more likely to look for other opportunities where they feel they will be valued.

- **Poor Performance:** When team members don't work well together, projects suffer. Missed deadlines, mistakes, and a lack of creativity are all direct outcomes of a fractured team.

- **Lack of Accountability:** When trust isn't present, accountability breaks down. People become more concerned with covering their mistakes or avoiding responsibility than with addressing issues collaboratively.

How to Get a Team to Bond

Bonding doesn't just happen—it requires deliberate effort. Leaders play a pivotal role in initiating and nurturing these bonds. The full, online TMS training curriculum has multiple lessons that detail the steps to quickly create a deep bond among team members. However, here are some strategies you can use now to help a team bond effectively:

1. **Start with Personal Connections:** Encourage team members to share personal stories, hobbies, or interests. This creates a deeper level of understanding and breaks down the purely professional walls that can separate people.

2. **Use Inclusive Language:** Shift how you refer to the team. Language creates reality, and when you consistently refer to "the team" rather than individuals or departments, you create a sense of unity. Speak about the "we," not the "he" or "she."

3. **Incorporate Team Building Exercises:** Incorporate activities that require collaboration and communication. These can range from structured team-building exercises to informal social gatherings where people can relax and connect outside of the regular work context.

4. **Define Roles Clearly:** When everyone understands their role and how it interfaces with other roles and connects to the team's overall goals, it fosters a sense of ownership and accountability. This clarity reduces friction between team members, as responsibilities are

well understood. Note: This concept is discussed further in step three of the *Truby Management System*.

5. **Celebrate Successes Together:** When the team achieves something—big or small—make sure it's recognized and celebrated as a collective victory. This helps reinforce the sense that everyone is in it together.

6. **Foster Open Communication:** Encourage an environment where team members feel safe to voice their ideas, concerns, and feedback. This openness prevents misunderstandings and fosters a culture of trust.

By implementing these strategies, leaders can create a culture where bonding becomes the norm, not the exception.

The Benefits of a Bonded Team

When a team is bonded, everything changes for the better. Some of the benefits include:

- **Enhanced Collaboration:** A bonded team works seamlessly together, supporting one another and leveraging each member's strengths to achieve the best outcomes.

- **Increased Innovation:** When people feel safe and valued within their team, they are more likely to share ideas and take risks. This kind of environment fosters creativity and innovation.

- **Higher Morale:** A bonded team is a happy team. When people feel connected to one another, they find more satisfaction and purpose in their work, leading to higher morale overall.

- **Better Problem Solving:** Teams that trust each other can handle conflict in a productive way. Rather than avoiding or escalating issues, bonded teams collaborate to find solutions together.

- **Reduced Turnover:** Employees are far more likely to stay with an organization where they feel connected to their peers. This sense of belonging reduces turnover and helps retain talent.

Key Points of Step One: The Power of Bonding

One of the most powerful transformations a leader can bring to their team is the ability to foster true bonding. Step one of the *Truby Management System (TMS)*—bonding—is where the journey toward creating a high-performing team begins. Without it, trust remains shallow, collaboration is forced, and teams struggle to reach their full potential. But when a leader focuses on bonding, everything changes.

Consider the story of an architectural firm's team that was fragmented and low on morale. The leader implemented the TMS, starting with **step one: bonding**, where the focus was on helping the team members get to know one another on a deeper level. They began using simple bonding exercises taught in the full TMS Training Curriculum and started referring to themselves as a **team** instead of just a group of employees. Small changes, like using team language and acknowledging individual strengths, created a profound shift in how the team worked together. Soon, they experienced higher morale, fewer mistakes, and better outcomes across the board.

This sense of bonding didn't just make the team more productive—it made them **want** to work together. They began supporting one another, stepping up to help when needed, and sharing in each other's successes. The result was not only a **more efficient and effective team**, but also a more **stable and sustainable one**.

Another example comes from a struggling healthcare clinic. Before TMS, the clinic faced issues with low morale and constant complaints. But once they focused on team bonding, the culture shifted. People started taking pride in their work, and the entire atmosphere changed. Labor ratios improved, complaints disappeared, and morale surged.

The personal benefits for leaders who implement bonding, supported by the rest of the *Truby Management System* steps, are immense. Leaders no longer spend their days putting out fires or dealing with interpersonal conflicts. Instead, they enjoy a **positive, engaged team** that performs at a high level. They get to lead, rather than micromanage. And as the team thrives, the leader often experiences a renewed sense of purpose and fulfillment.

These stories reflect the transformative power of bonding. It's a fundamental shift that leads to both personal and professional success. But bonding is just the first step. The full *Truby Management System* provides a roadmap for transforming not only your team but your entire organization.

As you are inspired by this primer on the TMS, know that the full training program (www.TrubyAchievements.com) offers even more depth and practical tools to handle the day-to-day challenges of leadership. From managing conflict and improving communication to increasing profitability, the full TMS equips leaders to build **high-performing, engaged teams** that drive success. Whether you're facing a troubled team or looking to enhance an already successful one, the *Truby Management System* can help you unlock your leadership potential and make your team a powerhouse.

But the journey toward a high-performing team starts with this crucial step of bonding, and leaders hold the keys to unlocking their team's full potential.

Chapter 7.

Step Two: The Power of Agreements in Team Dynamics

In any relationship—personal or professional—agreements form the bedrock upon which trust, cooperation, and accountability are built. In the context of high-performing teams, agreements take on even greater significance. They set clear expectations, align behaviors, and ensure everyone is on the same page. Step two of the *Truby Management System (TMS)* focuses on the importance of **agreements** as a fundamental tool to eliminate misunderstandings, foster mutual respect, and build a culture of accountability.

Just as bonding lays the emotional foundation for a successful team, agreements provide the structural framework that governs how the team operates. Without these agreements in place, even the most well-bonded team can falter due to confusion, misaligned goals, and inconsistent behavior. In short, agreements are crucial to building and sustaining a high-performing team.

Why Teams Fail Without Agreements

One of the most common reasons for team dysfunction is the absence of clear, mutually understood agreements. Here are several key causes that lead to this problem:

1. **Assumptions Instead of Clarity:** Often, teams operate on unspoken expectations, where team members assume others know what is required of them.
   This can lead to judgment, miscommunication, and disappointment when things don't go as expected.

2. **Lack of Explicit Guidelines:** When guidelines for behavior, responsibility, and performance are not made explicit, team members are left to interpret the "rules" based on their personal preferences or prior experiences, leading to inconsistent performance. Without clarity, all you have left are assumptions. Rarely do groups of people share the same assumptions on expected behavior and interactions.

3. **Unaligned Goals:** Without a clear agreement on what the team is working toward, individuals may pursue their own priorities, which can fragment team efforts and dilute overall success.

4. **No System for Accountability:** Without agreements, there is no fair and consistent way for team members to be accountable. As a result, some may not meet expectations, leading to frustration for those who are more diligent when the real problem is lack of clear and aligned agreements.

The Consequences of Poor or No Agreements

Teams that lack clear agreements face significant challenges that undermine both their day-to-day functioning and their long-term success. Some of the most common consequences include:

- **Low Morale:** When expectations aren't clear, team members may feel they are being unfairly judged or that they are constantly failing, leading to a decrease in motivation and job satisfaction.

- **Increased Conflict:** Without clear rules governing behavior and responsibilities, minor disagreements can escalate into larger conflicts, as team members are left to "guess" what is expected.

- **High Turnover:** Teams that function without agreements often experience higher turnover rates because employees become frustrated with the ambiguity and lack of direction.

- **Reduced Productivity:** When time is spent clarifying roles, responsibilities, and behaviors—things that should have been agreed upon at the start—valuable work hours are lost.

- **Blame Culture:** A lack of agreements often leads to a blame culture, where team members point fingers instead of taking responsibility for problems.

What Effective Agreements Look Like

In the *Truby Management System*, agreements are not just about rules. They are about creating a mutual understanding of how the team will function, communicate, and be accountable. The goal is to create **shared responsibility** and **clear expectations** surrounding team dynamics and behavior that everyone can agree on, leading to fewer misunderstandings and greater team cohesion.

Creating agreements is a powerful tool in and of itself, but there are various aspects of an agreement that make it effective – or not. For example, an agreement that is more like a platitude is rarely helpful. If you ordered a pizza and didn't tell the restaurant what type of pizza you wanted, and the delivery driver didn't give you any estimate about when the pizza would arrive, it would make for a very dissatisfying experience. In fact, blame or anger would be generated simply because there wasn't a clear agreement.

Agreements, then, need to be specific and measurable. "Agree to be a good team member," wouldn't be a very clear agreement. There is no measurable behavior for accountability or even a way to assess whether a team member is living up to the agreement. An agreement that went something like this, "Attend all team meetings," is something that is measurable, and attainable, and each team member can be accountable for his or her initiative.

In the full online Truby Achievements Training, there is a deeper treatment of the science and implementation of agreements. Over the years, Truby has gathered ten high-leverage agreements that eliminate and prevent people problems, or "those petty people problems" so many leaders have complained about. For this primer, you can use the following instructions to build some agreements in your team.

A well-structured agreement in the following areas can give a team something to align with and be accountable for:

1. **Roles and Responsibilities:** Clear definition of who is responsible for what. Each team member should have a clear understanding of their role, the expectations tied to that role, and how their work contributes to the overall goals of the team.

2. **Communication Protocols:** Agreements should outline how and when team members will communicate with one another. This includes how to handle disagreements, how to raise concerns, and how decisions will be made.

3. **Accountability Measures:** Agreements should define how the team will ensure that everyone upholds their commitments. This includes setting expectations for follow-through, feedback, and consequences for not meeting agreed-upon standards.

4. **Behavioral Norms:** Teams need agreements about behavior, including how to treat each other, how to give and receive feedback, and how to work collaboratively.

A key aspect of making agreements effective is that they are **mutually created and agreed upon**. This ensures that all team members are bought into the process and feel a sense of ownership over the agreements, which increases their commitment to upholding them.

Steps to Implement Agreements

Here's a general approach to implementing agreements within a team based on the *Truby Management System*:

1. **Hold a Team Meeting:** Bring the team together to discuss the importance of agreements and why they are critical for the success of the team. This step is crucial because it sets the stage for buy-in from everyone involved.

2. **Create Mutual Understanding:** During the meeting, discuss what the agreements should include. Ensure that everyone has a chance to voice their concerns, preferences, and expectations.

3. **Draft the Agreements:** Once everyone has provided input, work together to draft the team agreements. These should be specific clear, and cover the essential areas of team function—roles, communication, behavior, and accountability.

4. **Get Team Buy-In:** Before finalizing the agreements, make sure everyone agrees with them and is committed to upholding them. This is not a top-down process; every team member should feel that they have contributed to the agreements and individually own the team agreements.

5. **Post and Follow-Up:** Once the agreements are finalized, make them visible to the entire team. Revisit them regularly, especially during team meetings, to ensure they are being upheld. When necessary, modify agreements to reflect changes in team dynamics or goals.

Benefits of Team Agreements

When a team operates with clear agreements, the benefits are far-reaching:

- **Increased Trust:** Agreements create a sense of fairness and transparency, leading to greater trust among team members.

- **Higher Accountability:** Clear agreements make it easier for team members to be accountable because expectations are clearly defined from the start.

- **Improved Efficiency:** With clear expectations in place, teams spend less time clarifying roles and responsibilities, allowing them to focus on getting the work done.

- **Better Morale:** Team members feel more confident in their roles and responsibilities when they know exactly what is expected of them, leading to increased job satisfaction.

- **Reduced Conflicts:** With clear rules of engagement, disagreements are less likely to escalate into conflicts. Teams can resolve issues quickly and move forward productively.

Key Points of Step Two: Agreements - Why They Matter

The second step in the *Truby Management System*—**Agreements**—is essential for creating a cohesive, high-performing team. By establishing clear agreements, leaders can eliminate many of the misunderstandings and frustrations that lead to poor team dynamics. In a team where expectations are clear, accountability is shared, and communication is open, people are more likely to feel connected, valued, and committed to the team's success.

As a leader, your role is to ensure these agreements are not just words on paper but living commitments that guide the daily operations of the team. By doing so, you can eliminate many of the "people problems" that often plague teams and instead focus on achieving success together.

The first two steps of the *Truby Management System* are in the first phase of team development – **Transform**. When an architectural firm in Seattle, Washington went through these first two steps of the TMS, they realized a marked difference in the interaction of the team and their performance. Some of the 39 principals, who had worked together for decades, reported that they had a greater sense of bondedness with their fellow leaders. Some said, "I feel more grounded and confident on this team now that the expectations of team engagement are clear."

Let's move on to the next phase – **Organize** – where team member's roles and responsibilities are organized into a cohesive unit with an effective structure.

SECTION 3

TMS PHASE TWO: ORGANIZE

Creating Clarity and Accountability

Chapter 8.
Phase Two Introduction: *Organize - Creating Clarity and Accountability*

Once your team has bonded and built a foundation of trust, the next phase in the *Truby Management System* is **Organize**. Organization brings clarity to roles, responsibilities, and communication flows, which are crucial for moving from chaos to a well-oiled machine. You can have the most bonded team in the world, but without clarity, people will struggle to know exactly what's expected of them and how to contribute to the team's success.

In this phase, you will define roles and create an organizational chart that clearly shows who is responsible for what. This is more than just a title or a list of tasks—it's about understanding the purpose of each role and how it fits into the bigger picture. When your team understands not only their own role but also the roles of their colleagues, you create a system of mutual accountability. Everyone knows who to turn to when a problem arises, and there's no confusion over who's responsible for what.

Clarity breeds confidence. When your team has clearly defined roles, they can operate with confidence, knowing they are focusing on the right tasks and contributing in meaningful ways. This reduces stress, minimizes mistakes, and ensures that every team member is pulling their weight. With the expectations of each role clearly outlined, performance improves, and friction decreases. People know how their work fits into the larger goals of the company, and this alignment fuels motivation and efficiency.

The Organize phase isn't just about assigning tasks—it's about creating a culture of **ownership and accountability**. Every person on the team should feel a sense of responsibility for their work and be able to trust that their colleagues will uphold their end of the bargain. Organization empowers your team to operate smoothly, with each member playing their part in the overall success of the business.

Truby Management System Steps for Phase Two: Organize

- Structure
- Expectations

Chapter 9.
Step Three: Establishing Structure for a High-Performing Team

When it comes to building a successful team, structure is crucial. While bonding and agreements lay the emotional and operational foundation, structure provides the framework for how the team functions. In the *Truby Management System (TMS)*, step three—creating a clear team structure—is essential for defining roles, accountability, and responsibilities. Without a well-defined structure, even the most bonded and agreeable teams will struggle to work efficiently and achieve their goals.

Think of a team's structure like the skeletal system of the body. Without bones, the body would collapse, and nothing could function correctly. Similarly, a team without a clear structure lacks the organization and boundaries it needs to perform at its best. Step three ensures that every team member knows their role, who they report to, and how their work contributes to the overall goals of the team.

The Blue Angels fly tight and beautiful formations. It is an amazing high-performing team whose attention to structure is necessary for their very lives. However, the six planes used in the demonstration performance are only a small number of people in the entire team, which consists of 17 officers and over 100 enlisted personnel.

A team member whose responsibility was in radio communications for the team was asked, "What makes the Blue Angels such a success?" Without hesitation, he said "Teamwork." A follow-up question reveals an answer that is exactly the dynamics of step three in the TMS. He was asked, "What is 'teamwork' to this team?" Again, without hesitation, he said, "Everyone knowing their individual role, understanding clearly what is expected in that role, and the trust that they will perform exactly those expectations, perfectly, and on time."

Why Structure Is Necessary for Team Success

When teams lack structure, several common problems arise, including:

1. **Ambiguity in Roles:** Without clarity on who is responsible for what, tasks often fall through the cracks, or team members may duplicate efforts unnecessarily.

2. **Breakdowns in Accountability:** If there is no clear structure in place, it's difficult to be accountable because responsibilities are blurred.

3. **Inefficient Decision-Making:** When lines of authority aren't clearly defined, decision-making becomes slow and chaotic, as team members may not know who has the final say.

4. **Frustration and Conflict:** In a team without structure, frustration builds as roles and responsibilities are unclear, leading to confusion and potential conflict among team members. Boundaries aren't clear, which creates power struggles or missteps.

The consequences of a lack of structure can be severe: missed deadlines, wasted resources, and increased turnover due to dissatisfaction among team members. A well-structured team avoids these pitfalls by ensuring clarity, accountability, and smooth operations.

The Building Blocks of Team Structure

In the *Truby Management System*, team structure revolves around an **Organizational Chart (Org Chart)**. This chart doesn't just represent the people on the team; it outlines the **roles** they fulfill and the **lines of accountability** that connect those roles.

The most important thing to remember is that the org chart is not just a visual representation—it is a **working document** that the team refers to regularly. It is referred to as an "ownership chart." Every element of a team's operations is owned by a role. When something needs improving, if there is a glitch in a delivery, or if there is something that needs to be fixed – the question arises, "Who owns that?" Then the "accountability leader" for the issue at hand takes the lead in addressing the issue.

An org chart/ownership chart clarifies critical questions such as:

- Who is responsible for each area of work?
- How does information flow between different team members?
- Who has the authority to make decisions, and who reports to whom?

This dynamic tool allows the team to function efficiently by ensuring that each member understands their responsibilities and who they are accountable to.

In the *Truby Management System*, step two: agreements plays a pivotal role in creating alignment and mutual accountability within a team. This step goes hand in hand with step three:

structure. At this stage, team members agree to a role along with the responsibilities and expectations in that role. Establishing clear role agreements ensures that everyone knows the rules of engagement for each box on the org chart, from how tasks should be performed to how team members communicate and collaborate.

One success story that highlights the power of this step comes from a team that struggled with recurring misunderstandings and inconsistent performance. The leader of this team introduced "Team Structure"—a structured set of roles with mutually understood rules governing everything from areas of responsibilities to task ownership.

Before these role agreements were put in place, team members often complained about unclear roles and responsibilities. Tasks would fall through the cracks, and conflicts would arise over who was accountable for certain deliverables. These challenges created friction in the team and negatively affected their productivity and morale.

Once the Team Structure was introduced and clarified, the dynamic shifted. Clear expectations were set on issues like timeliness, ownership of tasks, and communication protocols. Everyone agreed on these new standards, and because they were mutually understood and accepted, the entire team began to function more smoothly. Blame culture disappeared as it became clear who was responsible for what. The ownership structure fostered an environment where every team member could be accountable without feeling micromanaged or overburdened.

The impact was profound. The leader found that conflicts diminished, morale improved, and team productivity soared. By implementing a clear team structure, this leader created a team that operated in alignment, reducing the amount of time spent on correcting misunderstandings and managing interpersonal conflicts. With everyone adhering to the agreed-upon structure and expectations, the team became more efficient, ultimately driving better results for the company.

Whenever there was a decision that needed to be made or problem that needed solving, the team learned to ask two questions: 1) "What is the issue?" – which created clarity and focus on what needed to be addressed, and 2) "Who owns this?" – which spotlighted the person who had the leverage in making a decision or solving a problem. The smoothness with which the team functioned made for a much healthier and happier environment.

This success story is a powerful reminder of how foundational structure is to a high-performing team. When leaders take the time to build this structure early on, they eliminate confusion, foster trust, and create a culture of accountability that empowers every team member to do their best work.

The Consequences of Poor Structure

If structure is not well-defined, or if the org chart is not adhered to, it can lead to significant problems within the team. Here are some of the negative consequences:

1. **Weak Information Flow:** When team members aren't sure who to communicate with or where to send updates, important information can be lost or delayed, hindering productivity.

2. **Lack of Accountability:** If lines of accountability are unclear, tasks may not be completed properly, or they

may be passed off to others, leading to confusion and inefficiency.

3. **Confusion About Responsibilities:** Without a clear structure, team members may feel unsure about their duties or the scope of their roles, leading to either underperformance or overextension as they try to cover too many areas.

4. **Team Dynamics Breakdown:** When roles and reporting lines are not followed, team dynamics can collapse. For example, if a team member bypasses their direct supervisor to escalate an issue to higher management, it undermines the authority of the supervisor and can lead to distrust within the team.

How to Implement Structure in Your Team

Establishing structure in a team is a process that requires clear communication and thoughtful organization. Here's how to implement structure effectively:

1. **Create an Org Chart:** Start by defining the essential roles within your team. These roles should focus on responsibilities, not people. For instance, in a small team, one person might handle multiple roles, but the key is to ensure that the roles themselves are clearly defined.

   For example, a furniture store might need roles like (1) Manager, (2) Salesperson, (3) Delivery Person, (4) Installer, and (5) Accountant. Even if only three people are available to fill these roles, the org chart must still clearly depict the responsibilities that each person takes on.

2. **Define Lines of Accountability**: Once the roles are outlined, draw the lines of accountability. Each person should know who they report to and who is accountable for them. The goal is to ensure that every role has **one clear line of accountability**, without confusing or conflicting directives.

3. **Keep the Org Chart Active**: An org chart is not a static document that should be tucked away and forgotten. It should be a **working document** that team members refer to whenever questions arise about roles, responsibilities, or accountability. Leaders should encourage their team to "work the org chart" by using it to clarify issues like information flow, decision-making, and problem-solving.

4. **Ensure Role Clarity**: For each role, make sure that there is a clear understanding of the expectations. Every team member should know their primary duties, the metrics by which their performance will be measured, and how their work fits into the broader goals of the team. *Note: Clarity of expectations is addressed in greater detail in step four of the Truby Management System.*

The Benefits of a Clear Structure

Implementing a well-organized structure brings numerous benefits to a team:

- **Increased Accountability:** With clear lines of accountability, team members know exactly who is responsible for what, making it easier to track progress and understand who is accountable.

- **Better Communication:** A structured team knows who to approach for specific information, leading to faster and more effective communication.

- **Improved Efficiency:** When roles and responsibilities are clearly defined, teams can operate more smoothly. There's no wasted time trying to figure out who's in charge of a task or which team member should take the lead on a particular project.

- **Enhanced Morale:** A well-structured team fosters confidence and reduces stress. When team members understand their roles and what is expected of them, they can perform their duties more effectively and with less confusion.

- **Stronger Team Dynamics:** When the team's structure is followed, relationships and trust between team members are strengthened. It ensures that everyone knows their place in the team, which minimizes conflict and promotes collaboration.

Key Points of Step Three: Structure – The Critical Role of Structure in Team Success

A high-performing team requires more than just good intentions—it needs a clear structure. Step three of the *Truby Management System* emphasizes the importance of establishing an **organizational structure** that defines roles, clarifies lines of accountability, and ensures smooth operations. By implementing a solid structure, leaders provide their teams with the clarity and direction they need to perform at their highest potential.

As you continue implementing the *Truby Management System*, remember that structure is not just about creating a chart; it's about **living by that structure**. Ensure that the org chart is an active part of your team's daily operations, and you'll create a system that supports growth, collaboration, and success.

One of the most powerful transformations in a team occurs when a clear structure is established. Without structure, even the most bonded and agreeable teams can fall apart due to confusion over roles, accountability, and information flow. In **step three** of the *Truby Management System (TMS)*, leaders are taught how to create an effective **Organizational Chart (org chart)**, which outlines roles, responsibilities, and lines of accountability. This step is crucial for ensuring that tasks are completed efficiently, decisions are made smoothly, and accountability is clear.

A success story that demonstrates the importance of **structure** comes from a **struggling hardware store**. The team was overwhelmed by inefficiencies—tasks were being missed, responsibilities were unclear, and team members didn't know who to turn to for direction. The owner/manager implemented step three of the TMS by creating a clear org chart. This chart clarified who was responsible for what, and that made it easier to assign accountability and manage workflow. Once the chart was in place, the team saw significant improvements in their operations. **Morale improved, errors were reduced,** and **team communication became clearer**. Most importantly, the store, with its various departments, became more productive and **eliminated the complaints** that had been piling up before the structure was implemented.

This success didn't come from working harder or adding more people to the team—it came from **organizing roles** and **clarifying expectations**. The structure allowed the team to focus on their specific tasks without confusion, and accountability was clear. When issues arose, the team simply referred to the org chart to determine who was responsible for the task, ensuring nothing was missed.

This story highlights the transformative power of creating a solid structure within a team. Step three of the *Truby Management System* offers more than just an org chart—it provides a clear foundation for effective teamwork, improved morale, and a smoother, more productive workflow. As this store discovered, establishing structure doesn't just streamline operations—it creates an environment where people know their roles and can perform with confidence.

Chapter 10.

Step Four: Clarifying Expectations with Role/Responsibility Sheets

Step three in the *Truby Management System* is about creating the structure within which a team can operate more effectively. The focus is on roles, though the obvious component needed for each role is an understanding of the responsibilities and expectations that accompany each role. Step four, **clarifying expectations**, is a more detailed look at how to do that – specifically using **role/responsibility sheets**.

Defining a role is not enough. Setting clear expectations for each role is also essential for any high-performing team. Without knowing exactly what is expected of them, team members may experience confusion, frustration, and a lack of direction. Step four of the *Truby Management System (TMS)* focuses on the importance of creating **Role/Responsibility Sheets** as a way to set these expectations with precision. This step ensures that each person knows their responsibilities and how their role contributes to the team's overall success.

By now, the team has already established bonding, created agreements, and defined their structure. Now, it's time to clarify what each team member is responsible for by specifying **roles and responsibilities**, a critical move that will prevent overlap, misunderstandings, and inefficiencies.

Why Teams Struggle Without Clear Expectations

When expectations are unclear, teams often suffer from a number of common problems:

1. **Ambiguity:** If team members are uncertain about their responsibilities, tasks may be left incomplete, or they may duplicate efforts, wasting time and resources.

2. **Confusion:** Lack of clarity can lead to confusion about who should handle specific issues, leaving team members to either neglect them or struggle to step in.

3. **Dissatisfaction:** Team members who don't understand what is expected of them tend to feel underappreciated or frustrated, contributing to low morale and disengagement.

4. **Accountability Issues:** Without clear expectations, it's impossible for someone to be accountable for their performance, which can lead to a breakdown in team dynamics.

The Role/Responsibility Sheet: A Tool for Clarity and Accountability

In the *Truby Management System*, the solution to this confusion is the **Role/Responsibility Sheet**. This tool outlines, in detail, the specific expectations, duties, and performance measures for each role. It is different from a typical job description, which often focuses on general requirements and qualifications for the job. Instead, a Role/Responsibility Sheet is a living, detailed document that clarifies the **exact areas of responsibility,**

performance expectations, and **lines of accountability** tied to a specific role within the team.

A **Role/Responsibility Sheet** includes the following key components:

1. **Title of the Role:** This helps to clearly identify what the role is called and its place within the team's organizational structure.

2. **Line of Accountability:** This section specifies whom the person in this role reports to and who is responsible for their work. Accountability is critical in ensuring everyone knows who oversees their performance.

3. **Purpose of the Role:** This explains the reason why the role exists and how it contributes to the team's overall success. It answers the question, "Why does this role matter?"

4. **Areas of Responsibility:** Instead of listing tasks, this section focuses on broader areas of responsibility, allowing for flexibility while still maintaining clarity about the main duties.

5. **Expectations:** General expectations of behavior, communication, and performance are outlined so the person in the role knows how to conduct themselves and interact with other team members.

6. **Metrics for Success:** This outlines how success in the role is measured, giving both the person in the role and their leader a clear way to assess performance.

The Difference Between Job Descriptions and Role / Responsibility Sheets

One key distinction between a **job description** and a **Role/Responsibility Sheet** is that a job description is more formal and static, usually associated with hiring and onboarding. It outlines what qualifications and general duties are required for a person in a particular role.

A Role/Responsibility Sheet, on the other hand, is specific and situational. It is created based on the team's current needs and outlines the actual responsibilities of the person in the role at that moment. It's not just about what the person needs to be (like a job description), but about what they need to do.

For example, a job description for a nurse might specify that they must have a valid nursing license and follow general nursing duties. However, the Role/Responsibility Sheet would clarify specific responsibilities for that nurse in a particular hospital unit, on a specific shift, and with a particular patient population. It offers details like how often to check vital signs, where to record information, and to whom to report findings. In essence, the job description provides the big picture, while the Role/Responsibility Sheet fills in the specifics.

The Consequences of Not Defining Expectations

When expectations are not clarified through tools like Role/Responsibility Sheets, several negative consequences are likely to follow:

- **Missed Tasks:** Responsibilities can "fall through the cracks" because no one is explicitly assigned to them.

- **Overburdened Team Members:** In some cases, one person may end up doing more than their fair share of the work because they feel responsible for tasks that aren't clearly assigned.

- **Blame Culture:** Without clear lines of accountability, team members may blame each other for failures or missed deadlines, leading to a toxic work environment.

- **Low Morale:** Team members may feel uncertain about what is expected of them, leading to frustration and decreased motivation.

How to Implement Role/Responsibility Sheets

Implementing Role/Responsibility Sheets involves a series of steps that ensure every team member has clarity on their responsibilities. Here's how to roll out this process effectively:

1. **Clarify the Team Structure:** Before creating these sheets, ensure that all team members understand the team structure. The org chart should clearly show lines of accountability, and each role should be linked to that structure.

2. **Draft the Role/Responsibility Sheets:** You can either assign the task of creating these sheets to the leadership team or a task group, or even have each person draft their own. The latter option allows team members to offer their perspective on what their role entails, which can then be synthesized into a final version.

3. **Review and Adjust:** Once the Role/Responsibility Sheets are drafted, each team member should review them to ensure they understand their responsibilities. This step involves a conversation between the leader and the team member to finalize the expectations and ensure buy-in.

4. **Ensure Accountability:** Make sure that once the Role/Responsibility Sheets are in place, they are seen as "working documents" rather than something to file away. These sheets should be referred to regularly to ensure responsibilities are being met and updated as needed.

5. **Revisit Regularly:** Over time, roles and responsibilities may shift due to changing business needs or team dynamics. Role/Responsibility Sheets should be living documents that are updated whenever necessary to reflect the current reality of the team.

The Benefits of Role/Responsibility Sheets

When implemented correctly, Role/Responsibility Sheets bring several significant benefits to the team:

- **Clarity:** Everyone knows exactly what is expected of them and how they contribute to the team's success.

- **Accountability:** With clear lines of accountability, it becomes easier for team members to understand their accountability trail.

- **Efficiency:** There's less overlap in tasks, and fewer things fall through the cracks, leading to greater efficiency and productivity.

- **Enhanced Morale:** Team members feel more confident in their roles because they know what they are responsible for, reducing stress and frustration.

Key Points of Step Four: Setting Expectations for Success

Step four of the *Truby Management System*—**Clarifying Expectations with Role/Responsibility Sheets**—is a vital step in building a high-performing team. By clearly defining each team member's responsibilities and creating a structured way to measure success, leaders provide the clarity needed for accountability and collaboration. This step prevents miscommunication, ensures tasks are completed efficiently, and fosters a culture of shared responsibility. With Role/Responsibility Sheets in place, teams are equipped to perform at their best, knowing exactly how they fit into the bigger picture and how their work contributes to the team's goals.

Step four of the *Truby Management System*—**expectations**—is where a team's performance truly begins to crystallize. Clarifying roles, responsibilities, and what is expected of each team member prevents confusion and sets a solid foundation for accountability. A compelling success story illustrating the power of step four comes from a company that struggled with ambiguity in its operations.

At this company, roles were loosely defined, and employees often didn't know who was responsible for what. This led to constant miscommunication, missed deadlines, and frequent overlap in tasks. Frustration built up as team members were unsure of their expectations, and conflicts arose over who should take responsibility for certain outcomes.

The leadership team realized they needed a change and implemented **step four: expectations** from the *Truby Management System*. They created detailed **Role/Responsibility Sheets** that outlined each team member's role, areas of responsibility, and the metrics for success. These sheets were regularly referred to, updated, and used as **working documents**, not just static job descriptions. This simple step had a profound impact.

Suddenly, there was clarity. Each person knew exactly what they were responsible for, and communication improved drastically. The team no longer faced constant confusion over who was accountable for what. Morale improved as employees felt more secure and understood in their roles, and productivity surged because tasks were completed efficiently and without redundancy.

Most importantly, the **Role/Responsibility Sheets** gave the team a reference point, which empowered them to operate autonomously. They could now BE accountable without someone having to hold them accountable. This allowed the leader to step back from constant oversight or micromanaging and focus on higher-level strategy. This shift not only smoothed team operations but also gave the leader more time to focus on growing the business.

This story showcases how clear expectations—when actively managed—can transform a team from one that struggles with ambiguity to one that excels in accountability and efficiency.

SECTION 4

TMS PHASE THREE: MOBILIZE

Turning Strategy into Action

Chapter 11.

Phase Three Introduction: *Mobilize - Turning Strategy into Action*

With trust established and roles clearly defined, your team is now ready to mobilize. This is where the rubber meets the road and where all the groundwork you've laid begins to pay off. In the **Mobilize** phase, you'll align your team around the company's core value—the unique offering that makes your business stand out from the competition—and set actionable goals that move your team toward delivering that value consistently.

But this phase is more than just defining what your team offers; it's about driving movement. Mobilization is the process of getting your entire team to move in the same direction, working toward clear, shared goals. This ensures that everyone's efforts are aligned with the company's vision and mission. No more wasted energy on tasks that don't contribute to the bigger picture.

The value your team delivers is what your customers truly care about, and it's essential that every member of your team understands this value and knows how their work contributes to it. When the team is aligned around this value, they can work more effectively to meet the expectations of your customers, clients, or stakeholders. In the Mobilize phase, you'll also set short-term and long-term goals that are specific, measurable, and achievable. These goals act as stepping stones toward your bigger vision and give your team the motivation they need to keep moving forward.

Mobilizing your team ensures that every effort is purposeful, and every action deliberate. It takes the clarity established in the Organize phase and uses it to propel your team into action. This is where progress happens. Every team member knows what they're working toward and why it matters, creating a focused and driven team that gets results.

Truby Management System Steps for Phase Three: Mobilize

- Value Delivered
- Goals

Chapter 12.
Step Five: Understanding and Delivering the Value

A common pitfall for teams and companies is that they often focus more on what they are **selling** rather than what their customers are actually **buying**. The difference between these two perspectives is significant. Most teams are skilled at delivering a product or service but fail to understand the **real value** their customers seek. Step five of the *Truby Management System (TMS)* is all about uncovering and aligning with this value. It's about shifting from a product-focused mindset to a value-driven one.

The Value Misconception

Many companies fall into the trap of believing that the value they deliver is synonymous with the product or service they provide. For example, a furniture store may think their value lies in the quality of their furniture. However, that's not necessarily the reason a customer chooses them over another company. The customer might value their fast delivery or exceptional customer service, their superior knowledge, or even their location more than the furniture itself.

Similarly, a hospital may focus on providing excellent medical care, but what their patients may truly value is the **care experience**, including timely service, empathy, and clear communication from the staff. The product or service is important, but the **value** that customers are actually buying is often related to the experience or benefit that the product or service provides.

Why Teams Struggle to Identify Value

There are several reasons why teams are in the dark when it comes to identifying the real value they deliver:

1. **Focusing on Internal Operations:** Teams tend to focus inward, perfecting the technical aspects of their service or product, without understanding what their customers actually value. This creates a disconnect between what the company thinks is important and what the customer finds valuable.

2. **Making Assumptions About Customer Priorities:** Teams often assume they know what their customers want, but these assumptions are rarely validated. For instance, a business may assume their customers value low prices, while in reality, the customers are willing to pay more for convenience or reliability.

3. **Lacking a Feedback Loop:** Many teams fail to seek direct feedback from customers to find out what they truly value. Without this feedback, the team is left guessing, which often leads to misplaced priorities.

Consequences of Not Understanding Value

When a team fails to align with the real value they deliver, several problems arise:

- **Missed Opportunities:** Without knowing what the customer values most, teams miss opportunities to enhance their service or product. For example, if a company assumes low cost is the most important factor for customers, they may miss the opportunity to charge more by providing premium, value-added services.

- **Poor Customer Retention:** If a company is not delivering the value that customers expect, it leads to dissatisfaction and customer churn. When customers feel they aren't getting what they truly value, they are more likely to go elsewhere.

- **Inefficient Marketing:** When a company markets based on features rather than value, their message often falls flat. Marketing a product's technical features may appeal to some, but aligning the message with the value customers want to experience is far more powerful.

How to Discover and Align with Your Value

To address this gap, the *Truby Management System* teaches leaders to **discover** the value their customers are truly buying and then align every aspect of the team's operations around that value.

Here's how teams can effectively discover and align with their value:

1. **Ask the Right Questions:** The first step in discovering value is to go directly to the source—your customers. Ask them what value they believe they receive from your service or product. Importantly, do not guide or influence their answers; instead, listen for themes in their responses.

For example, a printing company might ask its customers, "What value to you receive from our services to you?" The answer might not be the quality of the printing itself, but the speed and reliability of delivery. This kind of feedback is crucial for understanding the real value customers are buying.

2. **Align Operations Around the Value:** Once the value is identified, it's critical to align all team members and operations around delivering that value. For example, if customers value quick response times over product features, then every process—from answering phones to delivering products—should be optimized for speed.

   This also means shifting how you talk about your service internally and externally. Use the language of the value in your communication, marketing, and even within the team to ensure that everyone is focused on delivering the same value-experience.

3. **Track and Amplify the Value:** After aligning around your value, continually track how well you are delivering on that value. Gather feedback from customers regularly to see if their perception of the value you deliver is changing. Use this feedback to adjust and amplify the value you offer.

Example: The Mini-Mart Story

One of the best illustrations of this concept is the mini-mart story. Customers don't go to a **mini-mart** because it has the best products—they go because it saves them time. The value they are buying is time. Everything about a mini-mart is designed to support this value, from convenient locations to the small store layout to the quick checkout process. The value isn't in the product itself (the bread, soda, or chips), but in the ability to get in and out quickly without hassle.

Imagine a mini-mart where the checkout process is slow, or the aisles are cluttered. The store is no longer delivering the value of convenience, and customers will likely go elsewhere. This demonstrates how critical it is to stay aligned with the value your customers expect.

The Benefits of Delivering the Right Value

When teams and companies align with the real value they deliver, several benefits follow:

- **Increased Customer Loyalty:** Customers are far more likely to return to a business that consistently delivers on the value they expect. When the experience aligns with their needs, they feel satisfied and understood.

- **Competitive Advantage:** In industries where products or services are similar, aligning with the right value gives a business a distinct advantage. Customers will choose the company that best delivers the value-experience they want, even if other companies offer similar products.

- **Improved Profit Margins:** By understanding and amplifying the value you deliver, you can charge appropriately for it. Many businesses undercharge for the real value they are delivering because they aren't aware of that value. Once identified, teams can adjust pricing to reflect the premium value they provide.

- **Enhanced Team Focus:** Internally, when every team member understands the value they are working to deliver, it creates alignment and focus. This reduces wasted effort on non-essential tasks and increases overall productivity.

Key Points of Step Five: Aligning with Your Value for Success

The fifth step in the *Truby Management System*—**Value Deliverable**—is about shifting your focus from what you are selling to what your customers are truly buying. By understanding and aligning with the real value your customers seek, you can differentiate your business, enhance customer satisfaction, and improve profitability. This step in the TMS helps teams discover their unique value proposition and structure their operations to consistently deliver on that value.

Ultimately, this shift in perspective leads to long-term success and sustainability, as your team becomes more aligned with customer expectations and more effective at meeting their needs.

A powerful success story involving **step five, value delivered** in the *Truby Management System*, comes from a **marine construction company** that initially believed their value lay in providing quality work at a lower bid than their competitors. They operated under the assumption that clients chose them purely based on price. However, after consulting with Truby Achievements, they decided to ask their clients directly, "What value do you get from buying our services?" The feedback was eye-opening—clients consistently said that what they valued most was the company's ability to **manage risk** in high-stakes projects, such as underwater repairs and dam construction.

This shift in understanding led the company to re-align their entire business model around the value of **risk management**. They adjusted their marketing message, made risk management more visible in their operations, and trained their project managers to emphasize this aspect when interacting with clients. As a result, the company was able to charge more for their services because clients saw a greater return on investment from the reduced risks.

This change in focus didn't just improve their reputation—it **dramatically increased their cash flow, profit, and growth**. By aligning with their value with marketing messages and processes, they quickly grew to be the largest, most sought-after company in their industry across a wide region. The key to their success was not just providing a service but understanding and amplifying the **real value** their customers were buying. By doing so, the company experienced exponential growth, greater market attractiveness, and long-term profitability.

This story highlights the profound impact that aligning around your true value can have on your business. Identifying and delivering the value that customers genuinely seek can be the difference between struggling with low margins and thriving in a competitive marketplace.

Chapter 13.
Step Six: The Power of Goals in Achieving Team Success

One of the hallmarks of a high-performing team is the ability to set and achieve **goals**. After all, teams exist to work together toward a specific achievement. If there is no goal, what's left is a bunch of individuals doing their individual jobs. There is no synergistic aligned energy toward a common goal.

Goals provide direction, motivation, and a sense of accomplishment, creating a tangible sense of progress and success. In the *Truby Management System (TMS)*, step six—setting clear and actionable goals—is critical for keeping a team aligned, energized, and productive. This step emphasizes the need for both **short-term goals**, which offer immediate motivation and opportunities for celebration, and a **long-term visionary strategic plan** that ensures all efforts are aligned with the ultimate direction of the team or company.

Why Goals Are Essential for Teams

A team without a clear goal is like a ship without a destination—drifting without direction. Every leader, by definition, is leading their team toward something, and that something is always a goal. But setting goals is not just about establishing a target; it's about creating a roadmap for success. Here are a few reasons why goals are essential:

1. **Direction:** Goals give the team a clear sense of purpose, guiding their actions and helping them focus on what matters most.

2. **Motivation:** A well-defined goal provides motivation. It acts as a rallying point that unites the team and helps them stay committed, even when challenges arise.

3. **A Sense of Accomplishment:** Achieving a goal gives the team a sense of pride and accomplishment, reinforcing their confidence and fueling momentum for future successes.

The Importance of Short-Term Goals

While long-term vision is crucial, short-term goals offer a way for teams to **see and feel progress** in the here and now. Achieving these smaller milestones provides a psychological boost that keeps the team motivated and focused. Short-term goals should be set with two main criteria in mind:

- **Achievability:** These goals should be realistic and achievable within a relatively short timeframe, such as a month or a quarter.

- **Alignment:** Every short-term goal must align with the team's longer-term vision, ensuring that each small win contributes to the broader objective.

The Value of Celebrating Wins

An often-overlooked aspect of goal setting is the need to **celebrate success**. When a team accomplishes a short-term goal, it's essential to acknowledge and celebrate the achievement.

This could be through formal recognition, team events, or even small gestures of appreciation. Celebrations serve several important purposes:

- **Boosting Morale:** Recognition of success lifts the team's spirits and reinforces the value of their hard work. Individuals and teams hunger to be acknowledged, appreciated, and recognized.

- **Fostering Unity:** Celebrating together strengthens the bonds between team members, further solidifying their commitment to each other and the shared goals. The team has a sense of "**we** achieved **that!**"

- **Sustaining Motivation:** Achievements provide motivation for the next challenge, helping the team stay engaged and forward-focused.

The Necessity of a Visionary Strategic Plan

While short-term goals provide immediate focus and energy, they are most effective when aligned with a **longer-term strategic vision**. A visionary strategic plan defines the overarching goals and direction for the team or company, serving as a north star that guides all decisions and actions. Without this strategic vision, short-term efforts may feel disjointed, and teams risk losing sight of the bigger picture.

A **strategic plan** should include:

1. **Long-Term Objectives:** What does the team or company want to achieve in the next 3-5 years? These goals

should be ambitious but realistic, providing a clear sense of direction.

2. **Alignment with Core Values:** The long-term vision must align with the organization's core values, ensuring that the goals are not only focused on profit or growth but also reflect the team's culture and purpose.

3. **Integration with Short-Term Goals:** All short-term goals should be milestones that contribute directly to achieving the long-term vision. This creates a sense of continuity and ensures that daily efforts are contributing to something meaningful.

How to Align Short-Term Goals with a Strategic Plan

To ensure that short-term goals contribute to the long-term strategic vision, teams must follow a few key principles:

1. **Prioritize Goals:** Not every task is equally important. Prioritize goals that have the greatest impact on the long-term vision, ensuring that the team is always working on the most critical tasks first.

2. **Break Down Big Goals:** Large, visionary goals can often seem overwhelming. Breaking them down into smaller, more manageable short-term goals makes them less daunting and helps the team build momentum.

3. **Regularly Review Progress:** Teams should regularly assess their progress toward both short- and long-term

goals. This helps ensure that they remain on track and can adjust their strategies if necessary.

4. **Communicate the Vision:** Leaders must consistently communicate the long-term vision, ensuring that every team member understands how their work contributes to the broader goals. This fosters a sense of purpose and alignment within the team.

Benefits of Clear Goal Setting

When teams set clear, actionable goals, the benefits are significant:

- **Increased Focus:** Teams are able to concentrate their efforts on the most important tasks, avoiding distractions and minimizing wasted time.

- **Higher Productivity:** With a clear roadmap in place, teams can work more efficiently, knowing exactly what needs to be done and when.

- **Greater Accountability:** Goals provide a standard by which team members can be assessed for contribution and accountability, ensuring that everyone contributes their fair share.

- **Enhanced Team Morale:** Achieving goals, especially when celebrated, boosts morale and fosters a sense of accomplishment, keeping the team motivated to continue pushing forward.

Key Points of Step Six: The Power of Goal Alignment

Step six of the *Truby Management System*—**setting and aligning goals**—is a crucial component of building a high-performing team. By setting short-term goals that align with a long-term visionary strategic plan, teams can ensure that every action they take moves them closer to their ultimate objective. This combination of immediate wins and long-term focus keeps teams motivated, productive, and aligned with the broader mission of the organization.

A team that knows its goals and understands how each task fits into the larger picture is a team poised for success. Leaders must not only set these goals but also inspire their teams to reach them, celebrate their successes along the way, and continually align short-term efforts with the long-term vision.

A compelling success story for **step six: goals in the** *Truby Management System* comes from a **casino/hotel in Reno, Nevada**. The business was operating at a loss and in need of a turnaround. The leadership team implemented the *Truby Management System*, focusing specifically on setting clear, actionable goals. The team aligned around both short-term and strategic goals, with an emphasis on improving revenues and operational efficiency.

Within just one year of implementing structured, strategic goals, the hotel experienced a **30% increase in revenues**. The team worked collectively, motivated by the clarity of their goals and the steps laid out to achieve them. Each team member understood how their work contributed to these larger objectives, and as progress was made, the leadership celebrated each milestone. This ongoing celebration of small wins reinforced morale and kept the team engaged in the process of continuous improvement.

This example illustrates the profound impact that clear, aligned goals can have on a business, turning financial losses into substantial gains. Here's another example from a landscape architectural firm. The senior principal wrote the following when Truby assessed the success and sustainability of the *Truby Management System* 6 years after implementation. It took one year to implement all the components of the TMS because the firm didn't have many of the success principles in place. Notice how his team developed, and how getting some goals and direction from a VSP (Visionary Strategic Plan) became very profitable.

> "We were able to work with Truby Achievements over the period of a year, experiencing their Commonsense Leadership Training. The results have been astounding.
>
> **A new teamwork attitude in the office developed, resulting in greater accountability. There was clarity in the goals set by the office, and as a result, goals were achieved.** The office is now structured in a highly efficient and profitable manner. Most notably, there was **a new clarity in my own purpose for running a business**, something that I really never fully evaluated. Finally, we have fun. Work is an enjoyable, rewarding experience for the vast majority of us.
>
> As an added "bonus" **over the past 6 years, our office gross billings have increased 230% while the office has grown by only two people. While total payroll has increased by over 200%, profits have increased by 200% as well**. A focused vision has allowed us to maintain our workload, improve the quality of our work, and retain employees despite any downturn in the economy."

SECTION 5

TMS PHASE FOUR: OPTIMIZE

Laying the Foundation for Success

Chapter 14.

Phase Four Introduction: *Optimize - Achieving Peak Performance*

The final phase in the *Truby Management System* is **Optimize**, and it's all about refining and improving your operations to achieve maximum productivity and profitability. By the time you reach this phase, your team is bonded, organized, and mobilized. Now, it's time to take things to the next level by creating systems that streamline your workflow and make everything run more smoothly.

The Optimize phase focuses on two key areas: systems and continuous improvement. Well-designed efficiency systems are the secret to achieving consistent results with less effort. They ensure that tasks are completed in the most effective way possible, reducing wasted time, minimizing mistakes, and maximizing output. Whether it's how your team handles communication, manages projects, or delivers customer service, efficiency systems help you get more done with fewer resources.

But optimization doesn't stop with systems. The true mark of a high-performing team is their commitment to continuous improvement. Even the best systems can be refined, and even the most successful teams can improve. In the Optimize phase, you'll create a culture of growth where your team constantly looks for ways to get better. This could mean debriefing after projects to identify lessons learned, encouraging team members to share new ideas for improvement, or setting regular benchmarks to measure progress.

Optimization is what separates good teams from great ones. It's what allows your business to scale and grow, without the growing pains that often accompany expansion. By focusing on optimization, you ensure that your team's success is not just sustainable but scalable.

Truby Management System **Steps for Phase Four: Optimize**

- **Systems**
- **Continuous Improvement**

Chapter 15.
Step Seven: The Power of Efficiency Systems

In any business, **efficiency systems** are critical to success. They serve as the backbone of operations, ensuring that tasks are completed smoothly, accurately, and on time. Step seven of the *Truby Management System (TMS)* emphasizes the design and implementation of **efficiency systems** that improve productivity, profitability, and overall workflow. This step is not just about getting things done faster—it's about creating a structured process that makes work easier to manage, saves time, and, ultimately, makes your company more money.

The systems you put in place are like the gears of a well-oiled machine. When they function properly, your team can perform at peak efficiency, wasting less time on redundant or inefficient processes. This step is where the TMS brings everything together, turning your efforts into tangible, measurable outcomes.

Why Efficiency Systems Matter

In the fast-paced world of business, every minute counts, resources are finite, and there's always a competitor wanting to take your place. Teams that lack efficiency systems often face bottlenecks, confusion, and wasted effort. Here are some common issues that arise in businesses without well-designed systems:

1. **Wasted Time:** Without a streamlined process, team members might be duplicating efforts, searching for information, or redoing work due to miscommunication.

2. **Inconsistency:** When there's no standardized system, the quality of work can vary greatly, leading to mistakes or poor outcomes.

3. **Low Morale:** Frustration builds when team members are unclear about how to complete tasks efficiently. This often results in lower productivity and job satisfaction.

4. **Missed Opportunities:** Inefficient systems can prevent teams from responding quickly to new opportunities or from scaling operations smoothly.

How Efficiency Systems Increase Productivity and Profitability

By implementing well-designed efficiency systems, your team can significantly increase both **productivity** and **profitability**. Here's how:

1. **Streamlined Workflows:** With systems in place, tasks are broken down into clear steps that everyone understands. This eliminates confusion and allows team members to focus on their specific roles without worrying about inefficiencies elsewhere in the process.

2. **Cost Reduction:** Efficient systems help reduce errors, which in turn lowers costs. Mistakes in production or service delivery can be expensive, both in terms of time and materials. By standardizing processes, you ensure that tasks are completed correctly the first time, every time.

3. **Better Use of Resources:** Efficiency systems allow businesses to do more with less. Teams can handle greater workloads without needing additional staff or resources. This is especially critical for small teams that need to maximize their output without increasing overhead.

4. **Increased Profitability:** The end result of increased productivity and reduced costs is higher profitability. Efficient systems allow teams to complete more work in less time, which directly impacts the bottom line. Whether it's completing more projects, increasing customer satisfaction, or reducing waste, every improvement contributes to the company's financial success.

Here is an example of how an efficiency system helped reduce the cost of resources, specifically labor costs, time consumption, and product availability for customers in a hardware store. When an order of items was delivered to the store, it came in multiple "totes," (large plastic containers). Before the team designed an efficiency system, it would take two people approximately two hours to put the items from three totes on the shelves. After creating a better system, it only took one person about 30 minutes to do the same thing. The store managers went on to create efficiency systems for all of their processes, dramatically decreasing the use of resources, generating a smoother workflow, and increasing profits.

Sometimes, coupling the design of efficiency with innovative use of technology or equipment creates astounding, almost unbelievable improvements. Every year, a large commercial nursery in Delaware had to cover all the small plants that were in growing beds before winter hit. Until they built a better system, it would take a large crew of workers 2 weeks to accomplish this task.

When the team learned about the principles and processes taught in the TMS training about systems, they completely blew the old method out of the water. By using equipment and creating a new system, **two people accomplished the same task in two days**! It was a remarkable achievement, the benefits of which were realized year after year.

Creating and Implementing Effective Efficiency Systems

Building a successful efficiency system doesn't happen overnight. It requires careful planning and collaboration across the team to ensure that the system addresses the most pressing needs of the business. Here's how you can create and implement effective systems:

1. **Identify Areas for Improvement:** Begin by analyzing your current processes and identifying areas where inefficiencies exist. Look for bottlenecks, repeated mistakes, or tasks that take longer than they should. Prioritize systems that will have the greatest impact on your overall productivity.

2. **Involve the Team:** It's crucial to get input from the people who will be using the system. Collaborating with your team ensures that the system is practical and addresses real-world challenges. A successful system is one that everyone understands and supports.

3. **Design the System:** A good efficiency system is simple, clear, and easy to follow. It should include:

    - **A clear goal:** What outcome is the system designed to achieve?
    - **Inputs:** What triggers the system or starts the process?
    - **Outputs:** What should be the end result once the system has been followed?
    - **Sequential steps:** Each step in the process should be laid out clearly, with what needs to be considered or done at each step.

    One of the key indicators of an efficient system is its ability to operate without constant adjustments. If your system has too many branches or decision points, it might be too complicated and should be simplified. If the system seems complex, you might be looking at multiple systems mashed together into one. Consider breaking the more complex batch of steps into smaller systems.

4. **Test and Refine:** Once the system is in place, test it under real working conditions. Gather feedback from your team to identify any gaps or inefficiencies. Systems should be flexible enough to evolve as business needs change. Continuous improvement is key to maintaining high efficiency.

5. **Maintain Consistency:** The success of an efficiency system depends on everyone following it consistently. Once a system is in place, ensure that all team members are trained and understand how to use it. Leadership must also reinforce the importance of adhering to

the system to avoid maverick behaviors that could derail productivity.

The Benefits of Efficiency Systems

The benefits of implementing well-designed efficiency systems are far-reaching, impacting every aspect of the business:

1. **Smoother Workflow:** When tasks are standardized and processes are clear, work flows smoothly from one step to the next. This reduces stress and confusion among team members.

2. **Increased Job Satisfaction:** Employees thrive in environments where they understand their tasks and can complete them efficiently. Clear systems remove the guesswork and frustration that often accompany disorganized workflows.

3. **Higher Profit Margins:** As productivity increases and costs decrease, companies can see substantial improvements in their profit margins. Efficiency systems not only save time but also enhance the overall financial health of the business.

4. **Better Customer Satisfaction:** A company that operates efficiently is more likely to deliver high-quality products and services on time, resulting in happier customers who are more likely to return and refer others.

Chapter 15. Step Seven: Systems

Key Points of Step Seven: Efficiency Systems Make Work Easier and More Profitable

Step seven of the *Truby Management System*—**Efficiency Systems**—is the key to transforming how your team operates. By implementing systems that streamline tasks, reduce errors, and increase productivity, you can make your business more profitable and your team more efficient. Efficiency systems not only save time and money but also improve morale and reduce stress by making work easier to manage.

In short, this step of the *Truby Management System* helps you **make money, save time**, and **make work easier**. With well-designed systems in place, your team will experience smoother workflows, increased satisfaction, and greater overall success.

In one remarkable success story regarding **step seven: efficiency systems** from the *Truby Management System*, a **boutique winery** experienced transformative results after implementing well-defined efficiency systems. Before the system was in place, the winery struggled with disorganization, low productivity, and operational inefficiencies. Tasks would overlap, communication was unclear, and employees often wasted time redoing work or duplicating efforts. The winery knew that they needed a change to streamline their operations.

Once they began applying **step seven**, they identified and created structured systems for each aspect of their operations. They started by focusing on **high-leverage areas**, such as inventory management and customer orders. By refining these key processes, the team was able to eliminate unnecessary steps, improve communication, and ensure that every employee followed the same streamlined procedures.

Section 5. TMS Phase Four: Optimize

The results were immediate and powerful. **Productivity surged**, allowing the team to process more orders with fewer mistakes. With the clarity and consistency provided by the new systems, they also saw an increase in **morale and employee retention**, as staff members no longer felt overwhelmed or confused about their roles. Most importantly, the winery experienced a substantial increase in **profitability** as operations became smoother and more efficient.

This example demonstrates how **efficiency systems** can revolutionize not just how a team functions, but also the financial success of an organization. By applying structured, clear, and well-designed systems, businesses like this winery are able to maximize their productivity, reduce stress, and significantly improve their bottom line.

Chapter 16.

Step Eight: The Mindset and Practice of Continuous Improvement

In business, nothing stays the same. Without deliberate effort, systems and teams naturally decline. This phenomenon is known as **entropy**, a concept in physics that refers to the gradual decline into disorder. In the context of a business or team, entropy means that if no energy or effort is put into improving processes, systems, or relationships, they will inevitably deteriorate. This is why **continuous improvement**—the eighth step in the *Truby Management System (TMS)*—is essential. It provides the energy needed to prevent decline and foster long-term growth.

Continuous improvement is not just a process; it is a **mindset** that leaders must embrace and foster within their teams. It's about learning from successes, correcting mistakes, and creating a culture where everyone is actively engaged in making the organization better. Continuous improvement awareness and conversations shouldn't happen once a year or within the launch of a continuous improvement program. Continuous improvement should be a way of life.

Why Continuous Improvement Is Critical

Businesses and teams face two choices: **stagnation** or **improvement**. When teams do not focus on continuous improvement, the risk of repeating mistakes, declining quality, and losing competitive edge increases. On the other hand, organizations that are committed to continuous improvement enjoy the following benefits:

1. **Sustained Growth:** Continuous improvement helps maintain and expand a team's capacity to deliver high-quality results. Every improvement builds on the previous one, leading to compounding growth.

2. **Adaptability:** Teams that adopt a continuous improvement mindset are more flexible and able to adapt quickly to changes in the market, technology, or customer needs.

3. **Increased Efficiency:** Regular improvements help streamline processes, eliminate waste, and boost productivity. This leads to smoother operations and reduced costs over time.

The Continuous Improvement Mindset

In the *Truby Management System*, continuous improvement is not just something a team does—it's part of the team's identity. The core of this step is a **mindset** that seeks learning, change, and growth at every opportunity. This mindset includes:

1. **Learning from Successes:** When something goes well, it's important to ask, "How did we achieve this success?" By analyzing successes, teams can repeat and amplify the behaviors or strategies that led to those outcomes.

2. **Learning from Mistakes:** Mistakes are valuable learning opportunities. By asking, "What went wrong?" teams can prevent the same issues from occurring again in the future.

3. **Welcoming Feedback:** A culture of continuous improvement is only possible when everyone feels comfortable suggesting changes. Leaders play a critical role in creating a safe environment where feedback is welcomed, not feared.

How to Implement Continuous Improvement

Continuous improvement requires a structured approach, which includes creating systems for capturing insights, analyzing performance, and making informed changes. Here's how teams can implement this step effectively:

1. **Create a Feedback System:** Establish a formal process for team members to provide suggestions on how to improve processes, customer service, or workflow. This system should be easily accessible and encourage regular input.

   For instance, consider setting up a digital platform or a suggestion box that team members can use to share their ideas. Feedback should not only be collected but also prioritized and acted upon.

2. **Conduct Regular Debriefs:** After completing a project, reaching a milestone, or making an important decision, hold a team debrief to assess what worked well and what didn't. These discussions should focus on learning and improvement rather than assigning blame. This creates a culture where improvement is part of everyday operations.

3. **Celebrate and Learn from Successes:** Every success is an opportunity for continuous improvement. After achieving a goal, follow a structured celebration process. In the TMS, this includes:

    - **Party Factor:** Celebrate with the team to acknowledge the achievement.
    - **Recognition and Appreciation:** Publicly recognize the contributions of individuals and the team as a whole.
    - **Learning:** Analyze what went well and why, so the success can be repeated. Also, consider what didn't go well so you can adapt and adjust for a better outcome.
    - **Transfer Knowledge:** Share the insights gained from the success with other teams or departments that might benefit from it.

4. **Prevent Repeated Mistakes:** When mistakes happen, it's important to address the root cause. Document lessons learned and put systems in place to prevent the same mistake from occurring again. This could include refining workflows, retraining team members, or implementing new checks and balances.

5. **Prioritize Improvement Opportunities:** Not all suggestions or areas of improvement will be equally important. Develop a system for prioritizing improvements based on impact. Focus first on changes that will deliver the most significant benefits in terms of productivity, profitability, or customer satisfaction.

The Benefits of Continuous Improvement

When teams embrace continuous improvement, the benefits are profound and wide-ranging:

1. **Increased Efficiency:** Regular improvements to systems and processes streamline operations, allowing the team to work faster and more effectively. Over time, this reduces costs and increases overall productivity.

2. **Enhanced Team Morale:** Teams that are constantly learning and improving are more engaged. They feel empowered to contribute ideas and see the results of their efforts. This sense of ownership fosters a positive, proactive culture.

3. **Sustained Profitability:** Continuous improvement directly impacts the bottom line. By eliminating inefficiencies, reducing waste, and improving quality, businesses can enhance their profitability over time.

4. **Greater Customer Satisfaction:** As teams improve, the quality of their output improves as well. Whether a team is focused on delivering a product or providing a service, continuous improvement ensures that customers receive the best possible experience.

Key Points for Step Eight: Leadership Drives Continuous Improvement

The eighth and final step of the *Truby Management System*—**Continuous Improvement**—is what prevents decline and ensures growth. It's not just a series of actions but a **mindset** that leaders must foster within their teams. By embracing this mindset, teams can consistently grow stronger, more efficient, and more successful over time.

Leaders play a critical role in this process. They must model continuous improvement by welcoming suggestions, learning from both successes and mistakes, and creating systems that encourage everyone to participate in making the organization better. With continuous improvement, every step of the *Truby Management System* gets stronger, helping to create a team that continually adapts, grows, and thrives.

A remarkable success story highlighting **step eight: continuous improvement** in the *Truby Management System* comes from a **large organization in the healthcare industry**. The company was experiencing stagnation, and leadership recognized that while the team was capable, their systems were not evolving. Over time, operational inefficiencies led to mistakes and recurring issues, as there was no structured system for learning from successes or failures.

When the company adopted the **continuous improvement** mindset from the *Truby Management System*, everything began to shift. They implemented a system for regularly debriefing processes and projects—asking what went well and what could be improved after each phase. This allowed the team to **learn from their successes and mistakes** and create processes that prevented the same issues from happening again. Continuous improvement became an ingrained part of the company culture, with all employees contributing to finding better ways to work.

As a result, the organization experienced a marked **improvement in morale and efficiency**. Over time, their **error rate dropped significantly**, and they saved both time and money by eliminating inefficient practices. By focusing on continuous improvement, the company didn't just improve operations; they also **fostered a culture of learning and growth**, which helped them stay competitive and adaptable in a constantly changing industry.

SECTION 6

CONCLUSION

Chapter 17.
Putting It All Together

As you can see in this primer, the eight steps of the *Truby Management System*, implemented in four phases, is a logical flow. It is a commonsense approach to building the relationships, interactions, behavior, and performance of a group of individuals into a high-performing team.

I'm sure you notice – none of these phases or steps "stand alone." They all work together to as pieces that create the whole picture. You can't have efficiency systems work well, for example, if people don't have a sense of bondedness with each other and agreements on how they will interact with each other. You can't have continuous improvement if people aren't performing well already. "Continuous improvement," the eighth step in the *Truby Management System*, comes AFTER good performance already exists.

Further, there is a logic to the sequence of the steps in the TMS. We have found that it is very difficult to create goals (step 6) if the foundation of team dynamics hasn't been implemented already. Or…you can readily see that efficiency systems (step 7) can only be meaningful and effective if the team knows where they are going (step 5).

In the context of look the *Truby Management System* as a logical, sequential, commonsense approach to building a high performing team and fixing people problems, look at it in this verbiage.

Phase one transforms a group of individuals into a high performing team who become bonded (step 1) and agree to the "rules of engagement and interaction" (step 2).

Section 5. Conclusion

Phase two organizes that team by clarifying who is going to accept the assignment of each role needed to achieve the goal (step 3), and what is expected from each role's engagement (step 4). A sense of ownership, motivation, initiative and accountability emerges from this kind of "ownership chart."

Phase three mobilizes the team by them clearly understanding the product or service they are to deliver (step 5) AND, more importantly, the value their customer or client is expecting to receive (step 6). Further, the team has a clear direction – a strategic plan that helps them align toward a given direction. This translates into the team's clear understanding of their next goal on the path to success.

Phase four optimizes the team as they design efficiency systems to enhance a smooth workflow (step 7) AND practice the mindset of continuous improvement (step 8). This keeps the team (and company) competitive, productive, and profitable.

In its simplest iteration, The *Truby Management System* takes a group of individuals, organizes them into a high-performing team, and equips them with the tools and processes to abundantly achieve lofty goals.

It is a known fact, the biggest headache for leaders – the biggest problem that keeps them up at night – are people problems. But teams don't change themselves, leaders do.

We've found that teams fit into one of three categories: Dysfunctional, Stagnant, or Good Enough. The *Truby Management System* fixes your team no matter what state they are in. Implementing the TMS will FIX the dysfunctional team, IGNITE the stagnant team and GROW the good enough team into their next level.

This book shows you how to get started, however, as we stated at the beginning, it's a primer. You can get great results from implementing the self-help action items explained in each chapter. The FULL training of every detail of each step could not be addressed in this small book. If you REALLY want be deeply trained consider our full training curriculum online.

Get TMS Training Now
www.TrubyAchievements.com

And one more thing. We said that the biggest problem for leaders is people problems...it's also a known fact – the biggest problem for the people is leadership problems. If you implement what you've learned in this book and/or get fully trained with our online curriculum, you'll be doing your team a favor.

Section 5. Conclusion

Summary of the Truby Management System

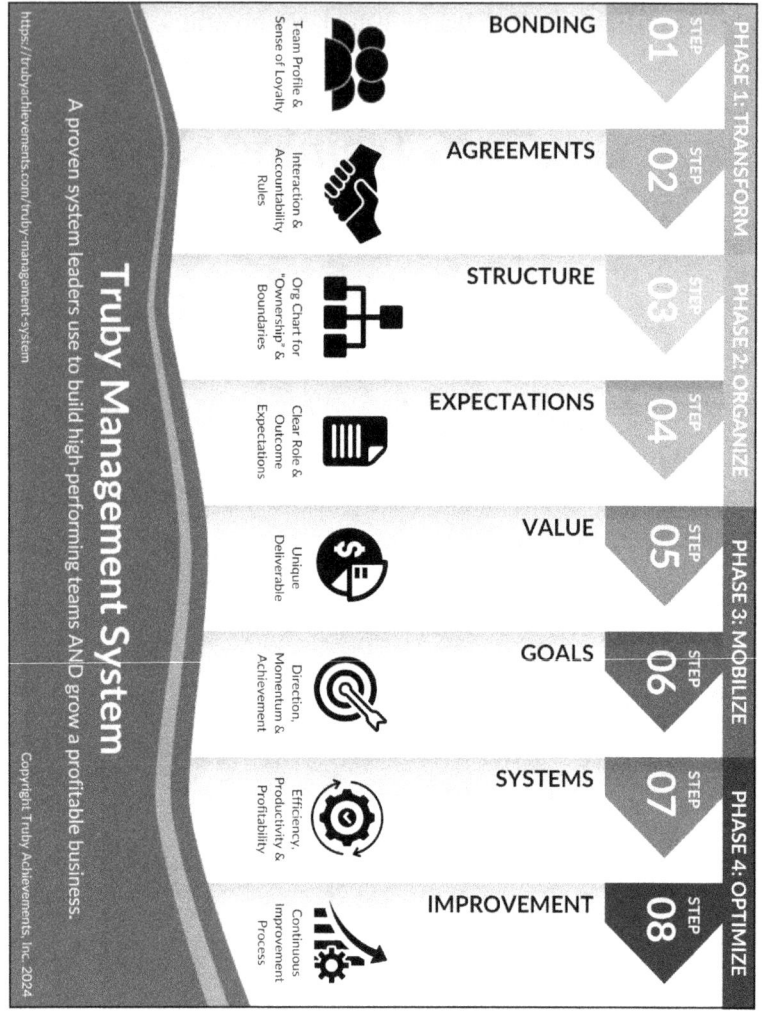

Chapter 18.
What's Next? How the TMS Can Help YOU

The *Truby Management System (TMS)* offers a clear, structured approach to creating high-performing teams and effective leaders. This book is a primer on the eight steps of the system, but there is a far more extensive **full training program** available. Think of this book as the first step in your journey. The full training is like earning an MBA, but better—it's practical, hands-on, and deeply rooted in the real-world challenges leaders face every day.

The online full training has been designed for people without much time. For example, you can learn everything you need to know to delegate successfully by watching a 9-minute video lesson. You learn how to ensure follow-through, how to handle the four reasons a person might not follow through, and how to make the dynamics of delegation a part of your team's culture.

Here is an example of how the Truby Achievements Training has a "speed-learning" aspect to it. A new member on the training platform decided to check out the practical, real-world tools and training. He was the owner of a small company and admitted that he did not know how to delegate successfully, so he didn't. He reported, "Since I didn't know how to delegate, I pulled up the 9-minute video lesson on delegation. I was pleasantly shocked that in 9 minutes, I learned how to delegate. The delegation flow chart showed me exactly what to do, the steps to take, and the important ingredients to stir into the delegation process. From that moment on I've been able to successfully delegate. That lesson changed my life."

Section 5. Conclusion

The full training is packed with lessons, tutorials, and tools that equip you to handle the diverse and complex issues leaders face on a daily basis. This is not just about learning theoretical models but acquiring practical skills you can implement immediately. As you master the eight steps of the *Truby Management System*, you'll find that your team starts to work more efficiently, your workplace becomes more harmonious, and your business runs more profitably.

This book is the starting point, giving you an overview of what the *Truby Management System* can do. But to **truly transform your leadership skills, fix troubled teams**, and **run a highly profitable business**, the full training is where you'll find the deep dive you need. Whether you're dealing with conflict, communication challenges, or operational inefficiencies, the full program covers everything you need to build a high-performing team and lead with confidence.

In the full training, you'll gain not just knowledge, but mastery in handling the most common issues leaders face, such as:

- **Team members who need to be accountable**
- **People who should take initiative instead of waiting to be told what to do**
- **Resolving conflict and improving team dynamics.**
- **Communicating with clarity and impact.**
- **Dealing with difficult personalities, including passive-aggressive behaviors.**
- **Running meetings that are productive, not time-wasting.**
- **Delegating effectively and creating accountability within the team.**

- **Building a culture that prevents gossip and encourages direct, honest communication.**
- **Wasting resources of time and money.**

This training will not only make you a better leader but will also result in immediate improvements in your team's performance and your organization's profitability. Leaders who have implemented the full *Truby Management System* report **faster results**, **better teamwork**, and **dramatic improvements in their bottom line**.

Now that you've had a glimpse of what the TMS can do, imagine what mastering these skills could mean for your team and your business. The full training is designed to give you every tool you need to build a high-performing team, fix a troubled one, or take an already successful team to the next level. If you're serious about leadership, the full *Truby Management System* training is your next step. Don't settle for just learning the basics—dive into the full training and unlock your team's potential!

The Transformative Power of the Truby Management System

The journey of leadership is not a static one. It requires constant learning, adaptation, and a commitment to growth. The *Truby Management System (TMS)* provides a comprehensive framework that equips leaders with the tools they need to create high-performing teams, streamline operations, and drive success. But more than just a set of steps, the TMS fosters a **mindset shift**—one that allows leaders to move from managing tasks to **leading people**, and from reacting to problems to **preventing them before they arise**.

Section 5. Conclusion

The success stories in this book are not unique. From Fortune 500 companies to small businesses, leaders who have adopted the TMS consistently report higher efficiency, increased profitability, and greater personal fulfillment. The magic of the system is its simplicity. As one leader described it, "It's not about doing more, it's about doing what you're already doing—**differently**." The system doesn't add complexity; it **simplifies** and clarifies operations, allowing teams to function more effectively and freeing up leaders to focus on the bigger picture.

As stated at the beginning of this book, **teams don't fix themselves - leaders do**. The *Truby Management System* will help with that. The benefits of TMS extend beyond just business outcomes. **Leaders themselves grow**, often discovering newfound confidence and competence in their roles. The system fosters leadership in a way that integrates professional success with personal growth, creating leaders who not only perform better but also feel more connected to their teams and mission.

As you finish this primer on the *Truby Management System*, know that this is just the beginning. The real transformation happens when you dive deeper—when you choose to implement the full training and master the system's tools, strategies, and mindset.

Training from the full *Truby Management System* curriculum offers comprehensive solutions to team issues, ensuring that leaders can build high-performing teams, foster positive cultures, and drive long-term success. By implementing the eight steps of the TMS, leaders learn how to address these common challenges effectively and sustainably.

The full TMS training program is not just about teaching you how to run a team or manage people—it's about giving you the skills to **lead with confidence**, create a workplace where your team thrives, and drive your business to new heights. Those who have taken this journey often say it's better than an MBA because it's practical, real-world, and designed to address the day-to-day issues leaders face. And some good news? Leaders who take this training consistently report that they get a huge amount of time back and they can finally have a personal life again.

If you're ready to go beyond this Book and take your leadership to the next level, the **Truby Management System** offers the comprehensive, actionable training you need. It's a system that has proven itself over and over again, for decades and thousands of team leaders, and it can do the same for you. Let this be the moment where you choose to transform your leadership, your team, and your business. The journey is worth it.

See Appendix A for a comprehensive list of what the *Truby Management System* **training fixes in teams.**

See Appendix B for rationale to use the *Truby Management System* **to fix in teams.**

Get TMS Training Now
www.TrubyAchievements.com

SECTION 7

APPENDICES

Appendix A.
Types of Team Problems *Truby Management System* Can Solve

The ***Truby Management System (TMS)*** is designed to resolve a wide range of challenges that leaders face when managing teams and running businesses. Here is a comprehensive list of issues that can be addressed through the training offered by TMS:

1. Leadership Challenges

- Lack of clear leadership direction
- Inconsistent decision-making
- Difficulty in creating trust and credibility with the team
- Micromanaging or lack of delegation

2. Team Dynamics

- Poor teamwork: Symptoms include blame, repeating mistakes, lack of initiative, and passive-aggressive behavior
- Lack of trust among team members
- Low morale and disengagement
- Resistance to change and innovation
- Toxic work culture driven by competition rather than collaboration

3. Communication Problems

- Miscommunication leading to errors and delays
- Ineffective meetings with no clear outcomes
- Third-party communication or gossip within the team

- Lack of open, honest dialogue
- Confusion over roles and responsibilities

4. Accountability and Ownership

- Lack of accountability for tasks and deliverables
- Team members not taking ownership of their roles or responsibilities
- Unclear expectations around job performance

5. Conflict Management

- Ongoing unresolved conflicts between team members
- Poor handling of confrontation, leading to festering resentment
- Passive-aggressive behavior undermining team efforts

6. Inefficiencies

- Disorganization and inefficiency in team operations
- Rework and duplication of tasks due to poor communication
- Time wasted on unnecessary meetings or unclear processes
- Inconsistent workflows across departments or individuals

7. Lack of Structure and Clear Systems

- Undefined roles leading to overlap or gaps in responsibilities
- No clear organizational structure, causing confusion on reporting lines
- Absence of systems for efficiency, productivity, and profitability

Appendix A.

8. Customer Value Misalignment

- Not understanding or delivering the value customers are truly seeking
- Focusing on selling a product rather than fulfilling customer needs

9. Profitability and Business Growth

- Low profitability due to inefficiencies and disorganization
- Struggles with scaling or growing the business while maintaining quality

10. Cultural Problems

- Poor or toxic workplace culture leading to disengagement
- Negativity towards leadership or company direction
- Internal sabotage caused by mistrust, gossip, or withholding information

11. Strategy and Goal Setting

- Unclear or unrealistic goals for team members
- Lack of alignment between short-term goals and long-term strategy

12. Personal Leadership Development

- Lack of confidence in decision-making
- Difficulty in managing stress or preventing burnout
- Challenges in personal growth and leadership development
- Unable to live a balanced life

Key Points Regarding TMS Team Fixes:

Many leaders struggle with persistent issues such as poor communication, unresolved conflict, passive-aggressive behaviors, and inefficient meetings. These are all challenges that arise when leading a team, and fixing them requires more than basic management skills. The Truby Achievements full training program dives deep into these specific areas, providing leaders with the tools and techniques to handle them effectively.

For example, conflict is inevitable in any team, but not all conflicts are handled well. In the Truby training, you'll learn a **four-step process** to manage and resolve conflict effectively. You'll gain skills in controlling emotions, clarifying the core concerns behind conflicts, and collaboratively working toward win-win solutions. You'll also learn how to prevent conflict by improving team communication, creating a culture where issues are addressed directly, and facilitating discussions that focus on solutions instead of blame.

Another major challenge leaders face is **clear communication**. Miscommunication leads to mistakes, missed opportunities, and frustration. The full training includes tutorials that teach leaders how to communicate clearly and ensure that everyone on the team is aligned with the objectives. You'll also learn how to deal with the personality differences that play out during any communication interaction, and how to prevent personality clashes.

You'll also learn how to hold **efficient meetings**—a vital skill for bringing people together, achieving consensus, and driving progress forward. Most people dread meetings because they often waste time and produce few results. But with the TMS approach, you'll learn how to hold meetings that are productive, concise, and goal oriented.

Appendix A.

Further, leaders often deal with team members who exhibit **passive-aggressive behaviors**, such as withholding information or subtly resisting collaboration. These behaviors erode trust and hinder teamwork. In the full training, you'll learn how to identify the root causes of passive aggression and how to address it in a constructive way, transforming your team into one that operates transparently and with mutual respect.

Another key focus of the full training is **meeting management**. Poorly managed meetings can drain energy, time, and resources from your team. Learning how to eliminate unnecessary meetings and **run efficient meetings** is essential for keeping everyone on the same page and ensuring decisions are made and followed through.

Appendix B.
Rationale for Using the *Truby Management System*

Tired of People Problems? The Truby Management System Is Your Solution

If you're like most leaders, you've probably spent more time than you'd care to admit dealing with **people problems**. Conflict, miscommunication, low morale, passive-aggressive behavior—the list goes on. These issues drain your energy, waste your time, and cause endless stress. You want to focus on growing your business, hitting targets, and achieving success, but instead, you're caught in the never-ending cycle of **putting out fires.**

What if there was a solution? What if you could **eliminate people problems for good** and build a team that works together seamlessly, delivering results day after day without the drama, frustration, or chaos?

That's exactly what the *Truby Management System (TMS)* does. It's not just another leadership course—it's a proven system that gives you the tools to **fix your team** and **eliminate people problems** once and for all.

People Problems Are the #1 Challenge Leaders Face—Here's How to Solve Them

As a leader, you know that **people problems** are your biggest headache. Whether it's personality clashes, poor communication, or team members not pulling their weight, these issues eat up hours of your time and keep you from focusing on what really matters. The worst part? Most leaders don't know how to **fix these problems**.

Sure, you can have tough conversations or offer pep talks, but without the right tools, the problems **keep coming back**. That's where the *Truby Management System* changes everything. With over 40 years of experience in transforming teams, Bill Truby has designed a system that not only solves people problems but **prevents them from happening in the first place**.

What the Truby Management System Can Do for You

Imagine leading a team where:

- **Conflicts are rare** and when they do happen, they are resolved quickly and constructively.
- **Team members communicate clearly** and openly, avoiding misunderstandings and wasted effort.
- **Everyone knows their role** and takes responsibility for their work, creating a culture of accountability.
- **Morale is high**, and your team works together as a cohesive, high-performing unit.
- **Meetings are productive**, focused, and actually lead to action—not just more talking.

The *Truby Management System* provides a step-by-step roadmap to make this a reality. It's specifically designed to tackle the **people problems** that plague leaders every day, such as:

- Unresolved conflicts and interpersonal tension
- Poor communication and misaligned expectations
- Low accountability and team members not pulling their weight
- Passive-aggressive behavior and toxic attitudes
- Inefficient meetings and unclear goals

With TMS, you'll have a **proven system** that fixes these issues at the root. Instead of spending your days putting out fires, you'll lead a team that **runs smoothly**, stays motivated, and consistently hits its goals.

Why the Truby Management System Works

What makes the *Truby Management System* so effective? It's designed for **real-world leadership challenges**. This isn't about learning abstract theories—you'll gain **practical tools** that you can apply immediately to see real change.

Here's how it works:

1. **Bonding:** Build strong team relationships that create trust and eliminate interpersonal conflicts.
2. **Agreements:** Establish clear expectations and mutual accountability, so everyone knows what's expected.
3. **Structure:** Create a solid foundation of roles and responsibilities, ensuring your team is aligned and operating efficiently.

4. **Expectations:** Clarify roles with **Role/Responsibility Sheets**, so team members know exactly what they're accountable for.
5. **Value Delivered:** Understand what your customers value most and align your team's efforts to deliver that value consistently.
6. **Goals:** Set clear, short-term goals aligned with a long-term vision to keep your team motivated and focused.
7. **Efficiency Systems:** Implement systems that streamline workflows, saving time and increasing productivity.
8. **Continuous Improvement:** Build a culture of growth and adaptation, ensuring your team keeps getting better.

Each step in the *Truby Management System* is designed to fix a specific leadership challenge. By following the system, you'll not only **solve your people problems** but also build a team that runs efficiently, meets its goals, and operates with high morale.

People Problems Don't Fix Themselves — Leaders Do

The reality is, **teams don't fix themselves**. If you're waiting for things to magically improve, you'll be waiting forever. People problems won't go away on their own, but as a leader, you can fix them—**if you have the right tools**. The *Truby Management System* gives you those tools.

With TMS, you'll:

- **Save time:** No more endless hours wasted on conflict resolution or chasing after team members who aren't doing their jobs.

- **Reduce stress:** Lead with confidence, knowing you have a system in place to handle any challenge that arises.
- **Increase productivity:** When your team runs smoothly, you'll see an immediate boost in efficiency and output.
- **Boost profitability:** With a high-performing team that consistently delivers, your business will grow faster, and your profits will soar.

Why Leaders Choose the Truby Management System

Leaders who have implemented the *Truby Management System* report **immediate improvements**. From struggling teams that turned into high-performing powerhouses to leaders who finally found a way to stop micromanaging and start leading, the results speak for themselves.

One leader said, "This system is **better than an MBA**. It's practical, it's real, and it addresses the actual problems we face every day as leaders."

Another success story comes from a large hotel and casino that saw a **30% increase in revenue** after implementing TMS. The key to their success wasn't a major overhaul—it was **fixing the people problems** that were holding them back.

Don't Wait—Take Control of Your Team Today

If you're ready to **eliminate people problems** and lead a team that performs at its best, the *Truby Management System* is your answer. This isn't just another management course. It's a **proven system** that will give you the tools to fix your team, save time, and dramatically reduce your stress as a leader.

The time to take control of your leadership and your team's success is **now. Don't waste another day dealing with people problems** that could be solved quickly with the right system or tool in place.

Take the next step toward becoming the leader you've always wanted to be. **Join the thousands of leaders** who have transformed their teams and businesses with the *Truby Management System*.

Get started today—fix your team, eliminate people problems, and lead with confidence.

Get TMS Training Now
www.TrubyAchievements.com

www.ingramcontent.com/pod-product-compliance
Lightning Source LLC
LaVergne TN
LVHW021829060526
838201LV00058B/3566